# Choosing and Using
# Climbing Plants

# Choosing and Using
# Climbing Plants

Barbara Abbs

LAUREL
GLEN

San Diego, California

**Laurel Glen Publishing**
An imprint of the Advantage Publishers Group
5880 Oberlin Drive, San Diego, CA 92121-4794
www.laurelglenbooks.com

All notations of errors or omissions should be addressed to Laurel Glen Publishing, Editorial Department, at the above address. All other correspondence (author inquiries, permissions, and rights) concerning the content of this book should be addressed to New Holland Publishers (U.K.) Ltd, Garfield House, 86–88 Edgware Road, London W2 2EA, United Kingdom. e-mail: postmaster@nhpub.co.uk

ISBN 1-57145-925-1

Library of Congress Cataloging-in-Publication Data
Abbs, Barbara.
    Choosing and using climbing plants / Barbara Abbs.
        p. cm.
    Includes bibliographical references (p. ).
    ISBN 1-57145-925-1
    1. Ornamental climbing plants.  I. Title.

    SB427 .A175 2003
    635.9'74--dc21

                                2002030099

Reproduction by Pica Digital Pte Ltd, Singapore
Printed and bound in Malaysia by Times Offset (M) Sdn Bhd

1  2  3  4  5  07  06  05  04  03

Senior Editor: Clare Hubbard
Editor: Jo Smith
Design: Peter Crump
Illustration: Coral Mula
Production: Hazel Kirkman
Editorial Direction: Rosemary Wilkinson

NOTE
The author and publishers have made every effort to ensure that all instructions given in this book are safe and accurate, but they cannot accept liability for any resulting injury or loss or damage to either property or person, whether direct or consequential.

Page 2: Boston Ivy, *Parthenocissus tricuspidata*, in glorious fall color.

Opposite: It can take a number of years before a wisteria produces its elegant clusters of scented lilac blooms.

## INVASIVE PLANTS

The following climbing plants mentioned in this book have become serious problems when introduced into certain areas. Check with your local nursery before introducing nonnative climbers, particularly in warm, fertile regions.

*Akebia quinata*
*Ampelopsis brevipedunculata*
*Anredera cordifolia*
*Cardiospermum grandiflorum*
*C. halicacabum*
*Euonymus fortunei*
*Ipomoea indica*
*Lonicera japonica*
*Lonicera periclymenum*
*Macfadyena unguis-cati*
*Passiflora spp.*
*Pueraria montana lobata*
*Thunbergia alata*
*T. grandiflora*
*Wisteria sinensis*

## GARDEN SAFETY TIPS

✱ When pruning, it is advisable to wear eye protection and gardening gloves. If pruning large hedges and trees, be careful when working overhead or from a ladder; if in doubt, call in a professional.

✱ When appyling fertilizers and weed killers, always follow the manufacturer's instructions, wear gloves, and wash your hands after use. Store safely in clearly labeled containers.

✱ Keep all tools and equipment clean and dry and store safely.

# Contents

# Introduction

ROSES, HONEYSUCKLE, CLEMATIS, AND WISTERIA are the names that immediately spring to mind when climbing plants are mentioned. Ivy, Virginia creeper, and sweet peas are the other popular climbing plants that everyone has heard of, but most of us would be hard-pressed to name any others. However, there are many other wonderful climbers that are less well known and deserving of close examination. Some are suitable for "problem" gardens and difficult places, and all can be used in a variety of ways. Unlike shrubs and perennials, which stay where you have planted them, all sorts of exciting things happen with climbers because they are constantly on the move.

Garden designers spend a small fortune on buying large trees to give instant height and maturity to a garden. Height in a garden, either from trees, surrounding walls, or from mounds and banks, gives a sense of scale and security. These features add an intermediate level between earth and sky. In some places, like prairie gardens or seaside gardens, the designer may want to create a feeling of being very small and insignificant in nature, but most of us prefer to feel enclosed and in proportion with our surroundings. For those who are impatient and lacking a small fortune, there is another way to create seclusion, increase interest, and add height to a garden–by using climbers.

Climbers are especially useful when creating a garden because most grow very quickly. A barren patch can be transformed in a season or two without enormous expense. Since the majority are fast growing, you can use climbing plants as permanent features or just as a temporary measure while shrubs and hedges are maturing. Climbers are versatile, too. Not only do they grow up, but they also hang down. Some can be trained into "standards," like wisteria and ivy, while others will happily crawl over the ground, disguising unsightly objects and festooning shrubs.

## HOW CLIMBERS CLIMB

Climbers are fascinating plants and they do not all climb in the same way. How they attach themselves to their supports affects how they can be used in the garden. There are four main types:

• Woody twiners are often referred to as *lianes* and are common in tropical forests. The long stems looping from tree to tree are familiar to filmgoers as the ropes that Tarzan swings from. Wisteria is the best-known woody twiner, common in gardens. Twiners have twining stems that twist around a support.

Left: The flowers and picturesque twining trunk of a mature *Wisteria sinensis* show up beautifully against the white paint and fresh green trim of this cottage.

Right: *Tropaeolum tuberosum* var. *lineamaculatum* 'Ken Aslet' makes a fine focal point, scrambling up an obelisk made of weathered wood.

• Tendril climbers support themselves by means of flexible tendrils that will twist around and hold on to anything they come across. They can have leaf-stem tendrils, where the stalks of the leaves twist around any likely support (for example, nasturtiums and clematis); stem tendrils, such as grapes and marrows; or tendrils derived from leaves, like the sweet pea and the Chilean glory flower (*Eccremocarpus scaber*). The tendrils of Virginia creeper (*Parthenocissus quinquefolia*) have tiny adhesive pads at their ends.

• Other climbers have adhesive roots that develop from the stems. These include ivy, climbing hydrangeas (*Hydrangea anomala ssp. petiolaris*), and *Campsis radicans*. Others have aerial roots, including the cheese plant (*Monstera deliciosa*) and the philodendrons.

• The last group of climbers include the roses (ramblers, climbing, and pillar roses), which hoist themselves through trees, shrubs, or man-made structures using their thorns for support. The tropical climber cat's claw vine (*Macfadyena unguis-cati*) has tendrils equipped with fine hooks that can penetrate the tiniest of cracks in brick and stone walls.

Then there is another group of plants, the scramblers, which are grown in the same way as climbers. These produce long, flexible stems that grow up through a neighboring shrub, then side branches that grow out sideways to keep the main stem from slipping down again. Blackberries and the winter jasmine *Jasminum nudiflorum* are good examples.

## ABOUT THIS BOOK

This book is a practical guide to choosing and using climbers. It opens with details on how to plant, train, support, and care for your climbers, followed by a useful section on selecting climbing plants for different soils and situations. For example, if you plan to erect a pergola on the north side of your house and you have acid soil, the plants you grow will be different from those chosen to clothe a pergola in full sun and in chalky soil. You may long for a glamorous wisteria, but if the conditions are not suitable, a flourishing climber of more modest appearance is preferable to a starved-looking wisteria with few or no flowers. You have to accept the limitations of your plot and work with them, and this is as true for climbers as for every other plant.

The book goes on to more aesthetic issues, with chapters on using climbers for color and designing with climbers. There are suggestions on how to make your garden appear larger by using certain colors, or how to choose climbers to create a romantic atmosphere. You will also find advice on using climbers in difficult places and for particular design problems, such as screening and creating focal points. The Classic Combinations chapter suggests ways to combine two or more climbing plants to complement and enhance each other to give you double the pleasure.

Even vegetable gardeners and indoor gardeners can find places for climbing plants. A shady corner in a vegetable garden can grow runner beans or gourds successfully and a hot conservatory can be shaded by using climbers that will thrive under the glass to create a leafy canopy.

The book ends with a directory of climbing plants, arranged alphabetically for easy reference. Here you will find details of all the fascinating plants mentioned throughout the book. Welcome to the world of the varied and versatile climbing plant.

*Campsis radicans*, the trumpet vine, is a self-clinging climber that will happily attach itself to walls or trees.

Roses, like this climber *R. Meihati* 'Sparkling Scarlet,' are shown to advantage on a pergola. In a tree, the thorns would hook on, but on a pergola it needs tying in.

A wild blackberry, a scrambler that uses prickles to cling to a host plant, grows with *Clematis vitalba* 'Old Man's Beard,' to make an unplanned but perfect fall partnership.

# CHOOSING AND CARING FOR CLIMBERS

*H*owever you want to use climbers, whether it is to screen, to veil, to draw attention to an object, or to frame a view, the plants need to be suited to the soil, climate, and aspect and require some care after planting. There is no need to be overly worried about caring for climbers; they require no more or less care than any other type of plant in the garden that you wish to flourish for a number of years. Selecting the right plant is essential. There are climbers for different soils, for sun or shade, and for different climates and positions. For example, honeysuckles are easy to grow with regard to soil and temperature, but are prey to aphids on hot walls, while clematis need their roots shaded, and most roses flower better in full sun.

The delicate yellow flowers of *Rosa banksiae* 'Lutea' and the bright pink of the thornless rose 'Zephirine Drouhin,' together with the wall shrub, a vivid blue *Ceanothus* 'Cascade,' make an eye-catching midsummer picture.

# Preparation and planting

EARLY FALL IS A GOOD TIME TO PLANT HARDY CLIMBERS, as the weather is generally mild and moist. However, if you are planting container-grown plants, you can plant at any time of year, provided the ground is not frozen. Bear in mind that if you plant in summer and the weather is dry, you must be prepared to water thoroughly every day using a two-gallon can of water. Tender climbers, such as passionflowers, are best planted in late spring or early summer, when the soil has warmed up. Before you begin to dig the soil, soak the plants well. The addition of seaweed concentrate to the water will help the roots to establish quickly.

## GARDEN KNOW-HOW

## Preparing the ground for planting

Soil preparation is vital to get climbing plants off to a good start. The soil beneath a wall can be very dry and often quite alkaline as a result of lime leaching from the mortar. If you plan to grow any lime-hating plants, it is worth doing a soil test.

1 Unless the soil has already been dug over or is well cultivated, dig a hole about 3 ft. square and two spits, or spade's depths, deep. Add a good quantity of organic matter, such as well-rotted farmyard manure or garden compost (A) plus two handfuls of bonemeal to the soil (B). If the soil is clay, add some lime to the subsoil (C). For very heavy clay, add peat, grit, or sand to open up the texture and mix it in well (D).

2 On very dry ground, soak the soil in the hole (E), then line the hole with lawn clippings, overturned grass patches (F), vegetable peelings, or other material from the compost heap. If you make your own compost and are not sure whether all the annual weed seeds have been killed, bury the compost at the bottom of the hole.

3 In chalk and sandy soils, add broken-up rotted grass patches and extra-bulky manures. Chalk soil will need liberal mulches added each year. If the ground is badly drained, line the hole with basic slag (G), brushwood, polystyrene, or even fiberglass.

**PLANTING**

The planting holes in the prepared soil need to be about 12 x 12 in. for most container-grown climbers and 18 x 18 in. for climbing roses. Put in any necessary stakes or supports when the hole has been dug. In very dry weather, fill the hole with water and let it drain away. Plant the plant to the same depth as it was in the container. Spread the roots out in the hole and cover with soil. Backfill the hole almost to the top, leaving a slight gap around the plant to help watering. Pack in the soil firmly and then soak again thoroughly with water.

After planting, mulch the area with chipped bark, gravel, or dry soil to retain moisture around the plant's roots. You will need to keep the climber well watered during the first season unless it is very wet or your soil is exceptionally retentive. One way of ensuring that enough water is carried directly to the roots of the plant is to insert a length of plastic pipe into the soil before you begin planting.

In the winter, after any frost, check that the plant's roots have not come out of the ground. If they have, pack them in again.

# Planting against a wall

Walls generally offer sheltered conditions for climbing plants and will help slightly tender plants survive outside. However, the position of the wall will make a big difference to the conditions it offers. Study your site carefully to determine how warm or sheltered the conditions are and how much light it offers, and choose your plants appropriately.

Be careful choosing plants for walls that get early morning sun. During cold weather when a frosty night is followed by a bright, sunny morning, frozen flower buds can be damaged if they thaw too fast. For this reason, choose plants that come into flower after the last expected frosts, such as roses or late-flowering clematises, including *Clematis* 'Duchess of Albany,' 'Ernest Markham,' or 'Hagley Hybrid.'

Do not dig the hole too near the wall—plant climbing roses and other vigorous woody climbers at least 18 in. away and guide the stems of the plant toward the wall with sturdy canes. Passionflowers (*Passiflora*), however, can be planted 8 in. from the wall, as they thrive in the dry conditions there.

1 Insert the stake firmly into the soil at the bottom of the hole. Keep the stake at an angle, leaning toward the wall, to guide the plant in the right direction (A).

2 Replace some of the prepared soil and pack it in well before you put in the plant so that it will be at the correct depth, which is the same as it was in its container or in the nursery (B).

3 Spread the roots out in a fan shape away from the wall. Any roots that are damaged should be cut off cleanly (C). Fill the hole, packing it but leaving a slight depression to help with watering (D).

# Training climbers

ALL CLIMBING PLANTS NEED SUPPORT, whether it is a tree or hedge, wall or trellis, pergola or wigwam. For annual or short-lived climbers, a temporary support is adequate, such as a wigwam of bean canes or a lightweight trellis. For perennial climbers, any wooden support should be sturdy and treated with a preservative. The poles should be set firmly in the ground, either in concrete or in metal post spikes, as the structure will need to last for many years and the plant may become very heavy. Walls should be in good condition. Some vigorous climbers, especially self-clingers like ivy or climbing hydrangea, may damage walls that have loose or crumbly mortar.

## PRACTICAL PROJECT

## Training plants on walls

Securing wires to a wall or fence is one of the easiest ways of providing support for climbing plants that need it.

1 Hammer vine eyes into the wall. They need to be spaced about 6 ft. apart and each row should be 20–24 in. apart.

2 Thread strong galvanized wire through one vine eye and, using pliers, fix it in position by bending about 6 in. of its length back on itself and twisting together. Take the wire through each vine eye until the whole length is complete. Allow another 6 in. and then cut the wire. Pull the wire tightly, bend it back on itself around the last vine eye, and twist together (A).

3 Attach the plant stems to the wires using plant ties, raffia, or soft string. Do not tie the stems too tightly (B).

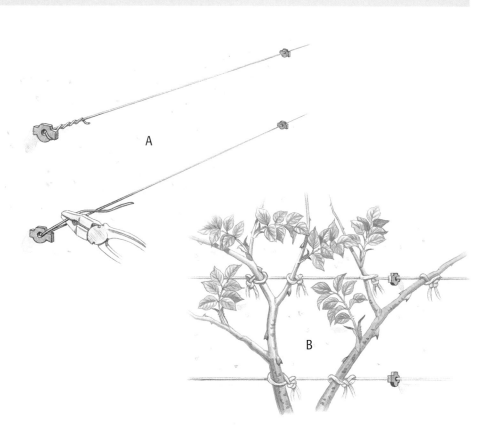

### TRAINING SELF-CLINGING CLIMBERS

Even self-clinging climbers, such as climbing hydrangea (*Hydrangea anomala ssp. petiolaris*) and ivy, take a little time to support themselves, so fixing them to the wall, fence, or pergola helps them to get established. As these fixings do not need to be long lasting, use plant hooks that are glued to the wall or a plant tie stapled to a fence–these should last in place long enough for the aerial roots of the plants to take over. Do not use *U*-shaped staples directly over the plant stems as they will soon restrict the stems' growth. Instead use the staples to fix plant ties or horizontal wires to the support and then carefully tie the plant stems in place.

### WALL SHRUBS AND WOODY CLIMBERS

Wall shrubs tend to lean away from the wall, so some support is beneficial. Likewise, woody climbers such as roses need strong and permanent support to guide them in the right direction. A good choice is flat or eyelet vine eyes embedded in the wall, through which wires are threaded. Good-quality trellis is another excellent option for roses and woody climbers.

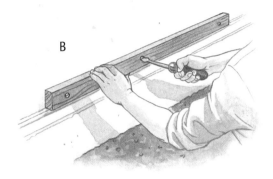

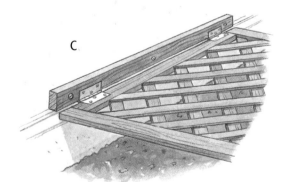

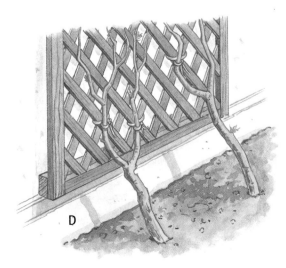

## Fixing a trellis to a wall

Attaching a trellis to wooden battens fixed to the wall allows for air circulation behind the trellis. If the wall is painted and needs regular maintenance, use hooks or hinges to attach the trellis to the fixed battens so that the trellis panels can be carefully folded down along with the plants while repairs are made.

1 Measure the trellis panel and work out where the top and bottom crosspieces of the trellis will go on the wall. Mark the place in pencil.

2 Cut two battens of 2 x 1 in. wood to the same width as the trellis panel. Drill holes in the battens at 18-in. intervals. Holding the battens against the lines marked on the wall, mark the positions of the holes (A).

3 Drill holes in the wall and fix the battens into place with screws and wall plugs (B).

4 Attach the bottom of the trellis panel to the bottom batten with a hinge fixing (C) and secure the top of the trellis to the top batten with hooks or a bolt fixing.

5 Finally, attach the plant stems to the trellis using plant ties or soft string (D).

### TWINING CLIMBERS

Some twining climbers will weave their own way through a trellis, but many, such as scramblers, will need to be attached. Do not attach the stems too tightly, and use a soft material. Wire can damage the plant stems, particularly with soft-stemmed climbers like clematis. Raffia and jute twine are good. Plastic adjustable ties and plant rings are easy to use but may be obtrusive. Strips of old nylon tights are ideal—flexible, soft, long-lasting, and usually an unobtrusive beige. Tie them neatly and trim loose ends.

For the curling leaf stems of clematis and other tendril climbers, a finer mesh needs to be added to the trellis. Different grades of plastic mesh are readily available and a 2-in. mesh is ideal. Simply fix it to the front of the trellis with staples.

# Pruning climbers

THERE ARE TWO MAIN REASONS FOR PRUNING. The first is to keep the plant in the place you want and to the size you want; the second is to improve the amount and display of flowers and leaves. Not all climbing plants need pruning–a vigorous climbing rose like 'Rambling Rector' or *R. brunonii* can be left to grow through a tree indefinitely, as can *Clematis montana* or Virginia creeper (*Parthenocissus quinquefolia*). However, in most gardens climbing plants need to be kept within bounds and they flower better and at a lower level if pruned regularly.

## How and when to prune

• **Plants that flower before midsummer on stems that have developed the previous year** Prune immediately after flowering. Prune about one third from each stem that has flowered, making a slanting cut just above a node (A).

• **Climbers that flower on new stems produced the same year** Prune in late winter or early spring before buds develop. Thin the stems if necessary, removing complete stems from near the base of the plant and cut out any dead wood. Cut the stems of very vigorous climbers back by about two thirds to keep them within their allotted space (B).

• **Evergreen climbers that are grown for their flowers** Prune immediately after flowering, cutting back to healthy buds (C).

• **Other evergreens** Prune in spring when there is no longer a danger of frost. Cut back dead or damaged branches to healthy wood and remove any other growth that is necessary to keep the plant shapely and in its allotted space. Established ivies can be trimmed over like a hedge. Where an ivy has reached the top of its fence or wall and has begun to spread out, cut it back hard in early spring using shears. You can do this every year. Virginia creepers can also be trimmed with shears when necessary (D).

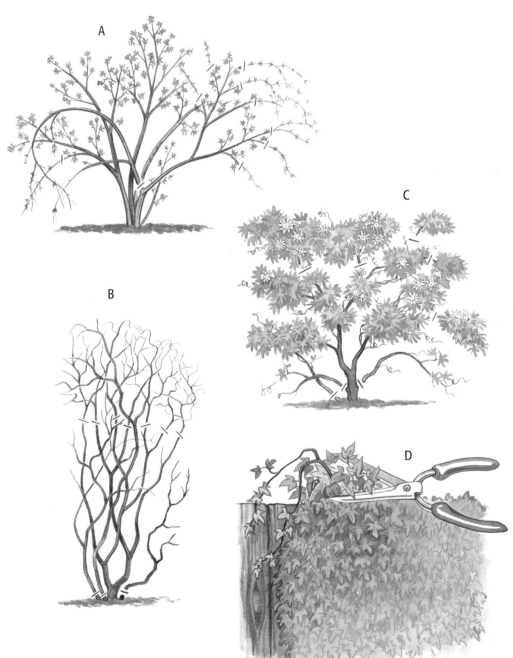

## PRUNING NEW PLANTS

Most new climbers should have their stems reduced by half, either when they are planted or the following spring (except for climbing roses). In the first spring, pinch out the tips of the growing shoots to encourage the plants to send out new stems from down low, creating a strong framework.

Do not prune climbing roses for the first two years. Many climbers are produced from bush-forming roses and may revert to their old form if they are cut back hard after planting. For more about pruning roses see pages 18–19.

To keep a honeysuckle flowering from top to bottom like this, prune after flowering.

## HARD PRUNING

Some climbers can be cut back hard to ground level. *Clematis viticella* and its cultivars should be pruned regularly in this way. For full details of how to prune clematis, see page 21. Other climbers that can be cut back hard include *Aristolochia*, *Campsis*, *Lonicera* (honeysuckles), *Passiflora* (passionflowers), and *Fallopia baldschuanica* (the Russian vine or "mile–a–minute" plant). Other overgrown climbers respond better to being gradually thinned out. *Parthenocissus tricuspidata* and other Virginia creepers can be cut back to stems no more than 2 in. in diameter and will sprout again. Honeysuckles can be cut down to about 6 ft. if they have been allowed to grow unhindered for a number of years; otherwise they need pruning after flowering.

# Caring for climbers

THERE IS NO NEED TO BE DAUNTED by growing and caring for climbers. The care of climbers is the same as the care of any other plant that you expect to last for a number of years. Below are some tips and advice on how to ensure that your climbers flourish.

## ROUTINE CARE

- **Feeding** For the first few years, apply a general fertilizer in spring. Pelleted chicken manure, seaweed meal, or a slow-release granular fertilizer are all clean to handle and easy to apply. Avoid using calcified seaweed meal if you are growing acid-loving plants.
- **Watering** All newly planted climbers will need regular and thorough watering in a dry year, just like other shrubs.
- **Mulching** Most climbing plants will benefit from regular mulching with well-rotted manure or compost each year in early spring. Apply the mulch when the soil is moist, adding a layer about 2 in. deep. The mulch will help retain moisture in the soil and will slowly break down into the soil to improve soil structure and fertility.
- **Winter protection** Many of the more colorful and exotic climbers are not fully hardy and may not survive a cold winter outside. There are many measures that you can take that will improve their chances of survival. The first and easiest thing to do is to mulch the roots heavily with anything you can get hold of, such as dry bracken, fallen leaves (which will need to be held in place with some form of netting), gravel, forest bark, coconut shell, or a proprietary mulch. Cover an area at least 24 in. from the base of the plant in all directions to a depth of about 6 in.

Wall plants can be protected by hanging straw matting from the wall over the entire plant. Alternatives are old curtains, rugs, bubble wrap, woven brushwood screening, or a cloche. If using any form of plastic sheeting, be sure to allow some ventilation. If possible, simply secure the material with bricks at the top and bottom of the wall. Remove winter protection as soon as the weather begins to warm up.

## COMMON DISEASES

### Powdery mildew

Clematises, roses, grape vines (*Vitis*), and honeysuckle (*Lonicera*) are particularly susceptible. Leaves and shoots appear to be dusted with flour. Spray regularly with a proprietary fungicide. If plants are growing in a greenhouse, make sure they have good ventilation.

### Black spot

This is another fungal disease that causes large, noticeable, dark brown or black patches on the leaves. Eventually the leaves turn yellow and fall off. These should all be carefully collected and burned. Use a proprietary fungicide every ten days, following the manufacturer's instructions. Some roses are resistant to black spot and if it is prevalent in your area, you may need to replace your plants with resistant varieties.

### Rust

Rust appears on roses as small orange pustules. Collecting the leaves and burning them is essential and you will also need to spray them with a proprietary fungicide. Many manufacturers produce a combination spray for roses to cure black spot, mildew, and rust.

### Clematis wilt

Clematis wilt is caused by a fungus that makes the whole plant collapse and die back at flowering time. It is very distressing but often the plant itself is not killed. Cut back the stems to ground level and spray with a copper-based fungicide. The plant may well shoot from the ground–if so, protect any new shoots from slugs. To keep wilt from occurring, plant clematises deeply.

## Honey fungus

Honey fungus can attack woody climbers, including wisteria. The fruiting bodies, golden or brown mushrooms, grow at the base. White threads can be found in the ground and under the bark. Plants deteriorate and eventually die. Dig out the plant, including as much of the root as possible, and burn it. Replace with a resistant climber.

## Cucumber mosaic virus

Cucumber mosaic virus, which can affect all cucurbits, affects passionflowers (*Passiflora*), stephanotis, and hoyas as well. Infected plants produce warty, distorted fruits, blotched dark green and yellow. Leaves are undersized and distorted with mosaic patterns of yellow discoloration. Infected plants need to be destroyed immediately.

**GARDEN KNOW-HOW**

## Getting a wisteria to flower

A wisteria grows quickly in its first years, producing plenty of handsome foliage, but often it will not flower until a woody framework has built up. This can take up to seven years in some cases, which can be a long wait for those seeking quick results. Follow the instructions here to encourage it to produce its elegant clusters of scented, lilac blooms as early as possible.

If the wisteria is not flowering after ten years, you may have a shy-flowering clone. You will have to face facts and either buy another plant and start again, or simply enjoy the leaves and twisted stems of the maturing plant.

1 Wisteria flower buds grow on short spurs, similar to apples and red currants. The aim of pruning is to persuade the plant to produce lots of short flowering spurs all along the main woody framework. Once the wisteria has covered the allotted space with woody branches, the new laterals that are produced each year should be cut back regularly.

2 Two months after flowering, prune the vigorous new growth back to 6 in. from the main branch. This can be done every two weeks throughout the summer.

### CARING FOR WISTERIA

Wisterias like a rich, medium loam. Where this is not available, ensure that the planting hole is half as big and half as deep again as suggested for other woody climbers and fill with enriched soil. Water heavily during the first summer. Wisterias last for many years and with a good start, need little attention after that except for pruning.

A wisteria needs lots of sunshine and a warm wall to help it flower well. In warm climates, wisteria can become a problem, as it can be invasive.

### ROOT PRUNING

Root pruning is occasionally advised for older wisterias that seem to be losing their flowering power. In early spring dig a trench around the wisteria about 18 in. deep and about 3 ft. away. Cut or saw the thick woody roots, being sure to leave the fibrous feeding roots untouched. Backfill the trench, firm the soil, and water well.

# Caring for roses

*ROSA* IS A VERY DIVERSE GENUS and some climbing roses will flourish with no feeding or pruning and remain free of disease and pests. Others are much less vigorous and demand a certain amount of pampering. A good mulch around the roots with manure in winter and two feeds per season with a proprietary rose fertilizer (follow the directions on the packet exactly; more is not necessarily better), will keep most roses happy. Many climbing and rambling roses revel in hot sunshine and warmer climates: 'Climbing Lady Hillingdon,' 'Marechal Niel,' 'Paul Transon,' *Rosa* × *beanii*, 'Royal Gold,' *Rosa banksiae*, *Rosa* × *fortuneana*, and 'Ramona' are just a few.

### CREATING THE RIGHT EFFECT

Small-flowered roses look more informal than those with larger, showier blooms. For a position near the house, choose a large-flowered rose like 'Altissimo' or 'Compassion,' but for a cottage-garden effect try 'Céline Forestier,' 'Pleine de Grace,' 'Dentelle de Malines,' or 'Madame Alfred Carrière.'

## PRUNING ROSES

Immediately after planting, cut back all the stems of roses to about 10 in. to encourage a good, strong framework to develop. The only exception to this rule is climbers that are naturally occurring mutations of bush roses; these should not be pruned for two years, as heavy pruning may make them revert to their bush form. After this initial pruning, adhere to the following rules, depending on the rose type.

• **Ramblers** After planting, a rambler rose may take three years to flower but it will form a good root system during this time. Do not prune for two years after the initial cutting back. After this, ramblers should be pruned each year in late summer after flowering. Ramblers can be divided into two groups. The first group consists of very vigorous growers that produce new branches from the base that flower in the second year. As old branches produce less flowers, they can be cut to the base after they have flowered in late summer or early fall and the new stems tied in (A). The second group, which are not repeat flowering, produce fewer new branches from the base; the old flowering stems should be cut back to a point where there is a strong replacement stem growing. Cut the stems back to the length you want them to be and then retie the stems to their support (B).

For a better screen, remove only a few of the older branches and cut one or two stems back hard to encourage new growth lower down. Many ramblers, like those that scramble over banks or through trees, need no pruning at all.

A

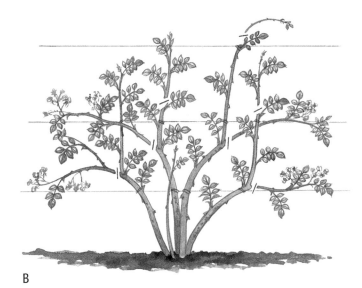

B

• **Climbers** Climbers produce their flowers on side stems and not on the structural branches. The structural branches should be trained immediately after the rose has been planted. Bend the branches to as near horizontal as possible without forcing them and tie them in place. Aim to create a balanced framework covering the designated area. Prune the flowering laterals each year by about two thirds, in late summer and fall (C).

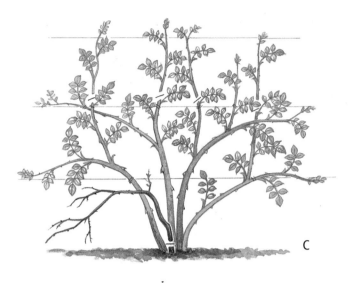

C

• **Shrub roses** Encourage shrub roses to flower over the whole length of their stems by fanning the stems out horizontally if you are planting them against a trellis or fence. Shrub roses need little or no formal pruning. Cut back any branches that are inconvenient or damaged in late summer, after flowering (D). If you are growing them over an arch or pillar, prune one or two of the main stems so that they are shorter than the others; allow some to reach their full height, one to be about 4 ft. tall, and another to be 24 in.

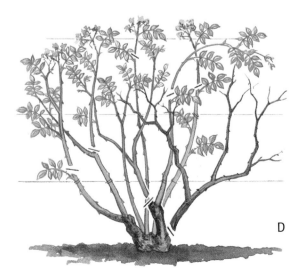

D

## ROSES FOR DIFFICULT PLACES

If the only place you can grow roses is in partial shade in difficult soil, such as heavy clay, very acid soil, drought-prone sandy soil, or strongly alkaline soil, try growing the species roses. These are the roses that have evolved naturally, and they are very tough. Choose from *Rosa pimpinellifolia*, *R. canina* and hybrids of it, *R. rubiginosa* and *R. rugosa*–'Blanche Double de Coubert' is a leggy white rugosa that can be used against a trellis.

Rambler roses are more successful than climbers in difficult soils, but the following tough cultivars are recommended:
'Climbing Cécile Brunner'
'Compassion'
'Constance Spry'
'Leverkusen'
'Madame Alfred Carrière'
'Madame Grégoire Stachelin'
'Maigold'
'New Dawn'
'Shropshire Lass'

The large clusters of intense pink flowers of *R.* 'American Pillar' can be overpowering in mixed company. Here, this tough and long-flowering rambler shows to good effect against different greens.

# Caring for clematises

CLEMATISES ARE AMONG THE MOST POPULAR CLIMBERS for temperate zones. The majority of species and cultivars are reliably hardy and sufficiently slender in growth to allow gardeners with small gardens to include several in their plantings.

You can find a clematis in bloom on almost any day of the year, and the range of colors is extensive. There are deep rich reds, yellows, almost blues, lavenders, purples, and whites, and they are borne either as eye–catching individual blooms or in pretty clusters. Some of the species are scented, like *C. rehderiana* and *C. armandii*. Others make fine ground cover.

## PLANTING CLEMATIS

Clematis likes a cool root run–in nature they grow close to rocks or from the bases of shrubs or scrub–and it is important to try to replicate these conditions. This is easily done by shading the soil area with a stone or with a few small shrubs.

Water the plants in their pots before you start to prepare the soil as described on page 10. If the soil is poor, replace it with a mixture of any proprietary compost, topsoil, and a slow–release fertilizer such as bonemeal. On heavy clay soils, add grit and sharp sand to help drainage. On a sandy soil, increase the compost or add some very well–rotted manure to the bottom of the hole. If you plan to grow two clematises (or any other climbing plant) in the same hole, make the hole twice as deep rather than twice as wide.

If the weather is very dry, fill the hole with water and let it almost drain away before planting the clematis. Plant the clematis with the top of the rootball 3 in. deeper than it was in its pot. Fill the hole almost to the top with the soil and compost mixture and then water again. Top up the hole with dry soil and then mulch well on top. If you like, insert a piece of pipe or plastic flower pot into the ground close to the plant roots to enable you to keep the roots, rather than the soil surface, thoroughly watered.

All clematises should be pruned back to the lowest pair of healthy buds in the first spring after planting to encourage them to become bushy at the base. Mulch each year in spring with well–rotted manure or compost.

*Clematis montana* is ideal for growing through a tree. Clematis should be planted at a distance from the tree trunk and guided toward it. It will need further support until it is well established through the branches.

# PRUNING

Clematises are usually divided into three groups that need different pruning regimes. Whatever your clematis, if you buy a plant from a nursery or garden center in full growth, do not prune until the following spring when all newly planted clematises should be pruned hard.

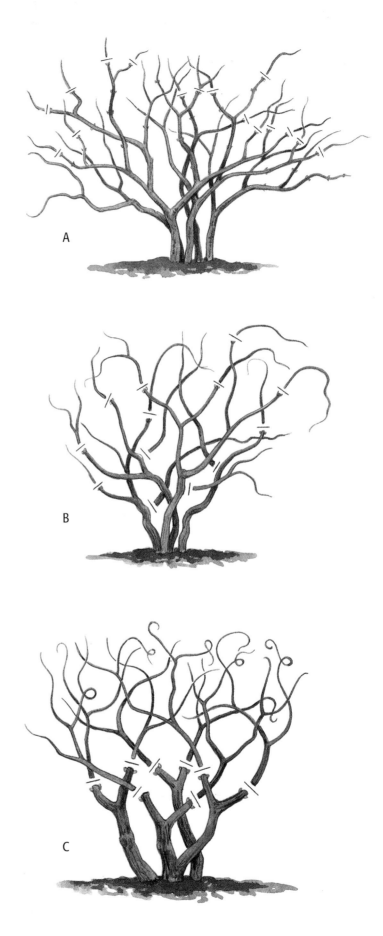

A

B

C

• **Group 1** (A) These are clematises that produce short flower stalks from the previous season's growth. They include *Clematis montana*, *C. alpina*, *C. armandii*, *C. chrysocoma*, *C. cirrhosa*, and *C. macropetala*. No regular pruning is needed. They only need tidying up as soon as they stop flowering. *C. montana* can be cut back hard if it has outgrown its space and this can be done a little later in the summer. Be careful when cutting into old hard stems, however, as the plant may die.

• **Group 2** (B) These are the early–flowering, large–bloomed cultivars, such as 'Belle of Woking', 'Duchess of Edinburgh', 'Nelly Moser', 'Beauty of Worcester', 'Marie Boisselot', 'Dr. Ruppel', 'Barbara Jackman', 'Daniel Deronda', and 'The President', which flower before midsummer. Prune back dead and damaged stems to a strong pair of buds in late winter or very early spring. On a wall or trellis these large–flowered clematises need to be tied in carefully to support the flowers, but if they are growing up a tree or shrub, this will probably not be necessary.

• **Group 3** (C) These late–flowering clematises produce their flowers in clusters at the end of the new season's growth. They belong to the Jackmanii, Orientalis, Texensis, and Viticella groups and include 'Hagley Hybrid', 'Niobe', 'Perle d'Azur', 'The Princess of Wales', 'Gravetye Beauty', 'Ernest Markha', 'Ville de Lyon', and 'Minuet'. In late winter and early spring, cut back each stem to just above the first pair of strong buds that you come to from the ground.

There are about a thousand clematis varieties available, with new ones appearing each year, so it is impossible to list each one and say how it should be pruned. Nursery catalogs and plant labels usually indicate which pruning group a particular clematis belongs to, so ask when you buy a plant. Remember, too, that it is not a disaster if you do not prune. The clematis will still flower, but not as well and often only on the higher branches.

# Choosing a climber

THE MAJORITY OF CLIMBERS will grow in any reasonable soil; most books recommend a moisture-retentive, free-draining, moderately fertile loam in sun or partial shade for most plants. Unfortunately these ideal conditions are the exception rather than the rule. Most of us struggle to grow plants in less than perfect soil and it is useful to know what climbers are likely to do well in the conditions and location we provide. There are some that must have an acid soil, while others do better in an alkaline soil. Some climbers will tolerate drought, others a damp soil.

Whatever the soil type or the location, prepare the soil carefully first, adding organic matter, such as manure, compost, or rotted grass cuttings, to increase fertility, aid moisture retention, and open up the texture. Most climbers will be in place for a long time and need a good start.

## CLIMBERS FOR ACID SOIL

If your neighbors grow heathers and rhododendrons, your garden probably has acid soil. It is worth buying a soil testing kit from a garden center to test the pH just to make sure. Acid soil has a pH of less than 7.

Asteranthera ovata
Berberidopsis corallina
Billardiera longiflora
Hydrangea seemanni
Kadsura japonica
Lapageria rosea
Mitraria coccinea
Mutisia oligodon, M. decurrens
Schisandra chinensis, S. rubriflora,
    S. sphenanthera
Tropaeolum speciosum

## CLIMBERS FOR ALKALINE SOILS

Most plants that will grow in alkaline soil do well in neutral or even slightly acid soils. Alkaline clay is difficult to work but is more fertile than thin chalk soil. Add organic matter to both when preparing the ground, but add several handfuls of coarse grit to the alkaline clay as well. Alkaline soil has a pH value greater than 7.

Actinidia kolomikta
Akebia quinata, A. trifoliata,
    A. × pentaphylla
Celastrus orbiculatus
Clematis sp.
Clianthus puniceus
Euonymus fortunei
Hedera colchica, H. hibernica
Holboellia coriacea
Humulus lupulus 'Aureus'
Hydrangea anomala ssp. petiolaris
Jasminum officinale
Lathyrus grandiflorus, L. latifolius
Lonicera
Parthenocissus henryana
Rosa sp.
Rubus
Schizophragma hydrangeoides,
    S. integrifolium.
Solanum crispum 'Glasnevin,'
    S. jasminoides 'Album'
Trachelospermum
Vitis coignetiae, V. vinifera 'Purpurea'

## CLIMBERS FOR HEAVY SOIL

Heavy, clay soils are often highly fertile but prone to waterlogging in winter and cracking in summer. Add plenty of organic matter and grit when planting climbers. Other materials that can be worked into the soil to help growth are coarse sand, ashes, manure, compost, and some lime. If the soil is a very heavy clay, consider replacing the soil in the planting hole with loam-based compost. Test the pH of the soil if you hope to grow acid-loving plants.

Ampelopsis
Aristolochia macrophylla
Campsis grandiflora, C. radicans,
    C. × tagliabuana 'Madame Galen'
Celastrus orbiculatus; C. scandens
Clematis (most species)
Decumaria barbara, D. sinensis
Fallopia baldschuanica
Humulus lupulus 'Aureus'
Hydrangea anomala ssp. petiolaris
Lathyrus grandiflorus,
    L. latifolius
Lonicera
Menispermum canadense
Pileostegia viburnoides
Rosa 'Albéric Barbier,' R. banksiae,
    R. filipes 'Kiftsgate,' R. 'Maigold,'
    R. 'Paul's Himalayan Musk,'
    R. 'Zéphirine Drouhin'
Rubus
Smilax rotundifolia
Solanum crispum 'Glasnevin'
Vitis coignetiae
Wisteria

## CLIMBERS FOR FREE-DRAINING SOIL

Climbers on the borderline of hardiness survive better in a well-drained soil, but many of these also need a high degree of fertility. Do not omit to feed and mulch plants in free-draining sandy soils. Check whether the soil is acid or alkaline.

*Anredera cordifolia*
*Campsis grandiflora, C. radicans,*
  *C. × tagliabuana* 'Madame Galen'
*Clianthus puniceus*
*Cobaea scandens*
*Cucurbita*
*Ercilla volubilis*
*Euonymus fortunei*
*Hedera*
*Holboellia coriacea, H. latifolia*
*Jasminum officinale*
*Lycium chinense*
*Muehlenbeckia complexa*
*Parthenocissus henryana,*
  *P. quinquefolia*
*Passiflora* (some species)
*Periploca graeca*
*Schizophragma hydrangeoides*
*Solanum crispum, S. dulcamara*
  'Variegatum,' *S. jasminoides*
*Trachelospermum asiaticum,*
  *T. jasminoides*
*Tropaeolum*
*Wisteria*

## CLIMBERS FOR COLD PLACES

Many climbers come from parts of the world where the temperature can drop very low, but survive because hotter summers ripen the stems well. In more temperate regions they may not flower or fruit as prolifically.

*Actinidia kolomikta*
*Ampelopsis glandulosa*
  var. *brevipedunculata*

*Apios americana*
*Celastrus scandens*
*Clematis aethusifolia, C. alpina,*
  *C. montana*
*Euonymus fortunei* var. *radicans*
*Fallopia baldschuanica*
*Hedera colchica, H. helix*
*Jasminum nudiflorum*
*Lathyrus latifolius*
*Menispermum canadense*
*Parthenocissus quinquefolia*
*Rosa canina, R. setigera*
*Rubus fruticosus laciniatus,*
  *R. phoenicolasius*
*Schisandra chinensis*
*Tripterygium regelii*
*Vitis amurensis, V.* 'Brant,'
  *V. coignetiae, V. labrusca*
  'Concord,' *V. vinifera* 'Ciotat'
*Wisteria floribunda*

## CLIMBERS FOR SHADE

While plants usually need sun to flower well, honeysuckles and some leafy climbers prefer shade.

*Euonymus fortunei*
*Fallopia baldschuanica*
  × *Fatshedera lizei*
*Hedera*

Climbing hydrangea
*Hydrangea anomala ssp. petiolaris*

*Hydrangea anomala ssp. petiolaris*
*Lonicera brownii, L. × heckrottii,*
  *L. sempervirens, L. × italica,*
  *L. × tellmanniana,*
*Parthenocissus henryana,*
  *P. tricuspidata* 'Lowii'
*Pileostegia viburnoides*
*Rosa* 'Félicité Perpétue,' *R.* 'Madame
  Alfred Carrière,' *R.* 'Madame
  Grégoire Staechelin,' *R.* 'Mermaid'
*Tropaeolum speciosum*

## CLIMBERS FOR COASTAL GARDENS

Salt-laden winds are a problem in coastal gardens but there are some climbers that can withstand them.

*Actinidia arguta*
*Campsis radicans*
*Clematis indivisa, C. montana*
*Fallopia baldschuanica*
*Hibbertia scandens*
*Hydrangea anomala ssp. petiolaris*
*Muehlenbeckia complexa*
*Parthenocissus tricuspidata,*
  *P. t.* 'Lowii'
*Smilax lanceolata*
*Vitis labrusca*

Boston Ivy
*Parthenocissus tricuspidata*

# COLORING WITH CLIMBERS

*F*or many people, flower color is what makes a garden. This is especially true in parts of the world where winters are damp and gray and light levels are low. The gentle sunlight, even in summer, makes some colors appear harsh. People long for color but feel uneasy about using it—too often a colorful garden can be a confusing glare of competing shades. Frequently, too, people forget to include what may be the main color of the garden, the bright green of grass, when they are designing their color schemes.

In contrast, in hot climates the brilliant sunshine makes bright colors look vivid and alive. The flame-orange Pyrostegia venusta that will cover a chain-link fence to such brilliant effect in Australia, or the vivid magenta bougainvillea that swamps white painted cottages in Greece, look brash in soft light and, anyway, need a greenhouse to flower really well.

*C. Tropaeolum speciosum* has vivid red flowers in late summer and is displayed to perfection against a yew hedge.

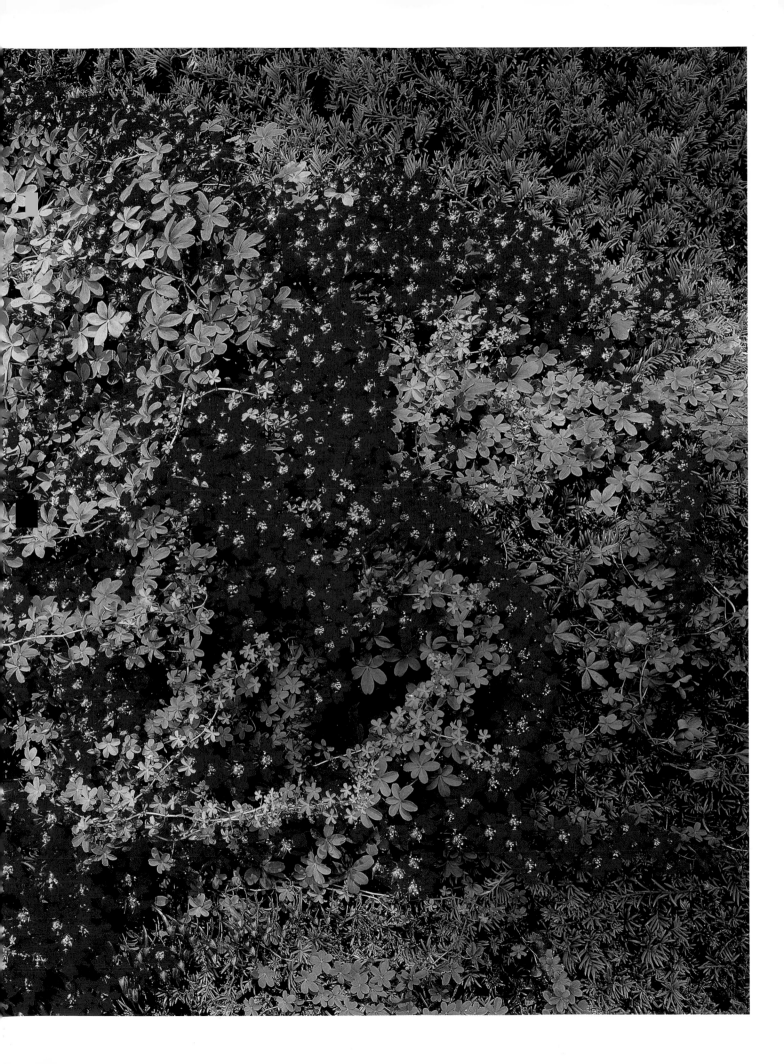

# Using color

IF YOU WANT YOUR GARDEN TO LOOK EXCITING, classical, romantic, or simply bigger, then color can do it for you, and climbers will do it quicker than any shrub. Colors can create many effects in the garden–you can cool an arid garden or cheer up a shady one just by choosing colors carefully.

   If you want to make the bottom of your garden seem further away, then plant climbers in receding colors such as soft blue or mauve. For a garden where the view is particularly important, the coloring can continue the scene. For example, in a seaside garden, keep to the colors of the sea and use complementary colors sparingly. Brilliantly colored climbers at the end of the garden in front of a view will bring the eye to a stop and spoil the effect, whereas some gentle greens will lead the eye on.

## COLOR AND SPACE

There are some simple axioms that are always worth keeping in mind when planning the colors of your garden:

• White flowers jump forward and appear to be closer than they really are, particularly in full sunlight. Use them to highlight attractive features or elements you want to display.

• White and pale flowers will appear to glow in shade; they can be used to brighten dark corners effectively.

• Deep colors, such as dark red and purple, create "holes" in the planting. They appear to recede into the foliage.

• Soft blues and grays look further away than they really are and add to the apparent distance. Use these colors at the bottom of a small garden to make the garden appear larger.

• Hot, strong colors, such as scarlet, orange, and yellow appear to reduce distance and look closer than they really are.

*Clematis* 'Duchess of Edinburgh' leaps out of the picture, taking the attention from *Solanum crispum* 'Glasnevin,' which, on its own, is quite an eye-catcher, too. Later, when the clematis has finished flowering, the solanum will come into its own.

## DESIGNING WITH COLOR

The natural landscape is usually made up of one color, or a harmony of colors over a wide area, like a bluebell wood or a fall scene. If there are many colors together, as there may be in a meadow, then the colors are like a kaleidoscope with shifting blues, reds, and yellows harmonized among the dominant green of the grass. Both these scenarios create a pleasing and subtle effect.

   However, if those same colors are separated into dense blocks or drifts as they may be in garden plantings, the individual colors start to compete with each other, all trying to claim attention at once. This can be exciting in the right surroundings, for example in a public park, but not in a garden designed to be a place of peace and tranquillity.

There are three main ways of designing with color in the garden:

• **The Italian method** In brilliant light an Italian garden can seem almost black and white, with dark evergreens and pale stone. There is just a small amount of brilliant color, with a few pots and tubs of flowers.

• **The natural way** Nature keeps one color or a harmony of colors dominant over a wide area or, if there are lots of colors, they are broken up into kaleidoscope patterns.

• **Using plants like paints** This idea uses color more deliberately and artistically. Gertrude Jekyll did this in the early part of the twentieth century in England, using subtle progressions of color, for example from pale blue to white to pale yellow and pink, then through the yellows to orange and red. The colors are strong in the center of the bed, but "in good harmonies, never garish." In South America, Roberto Burle Marx designed gardens and flower beds made up of bold shapes in vivid contrasting colors, which look like modern paintings.

## THE COLOR WHEEL

The color wheel, or color circle, was devised in the mid-nineteenth century and the colors are arranged so that complementary colors fall opposite to each other. Many designers and flower arrangers find this helpful in planning their color schemes and it can be used to plan a border, too.

## Complementary colors

These are the colors that fall opposite to each other in the color wheel, such as red and green, purple and orange, or blue and yellow. When used together in a color scheme, each heightens the effect of the other. For example, the pink of almond blossom in spring looks better when seen against a gray-blue conifer than it does against the bright green of young leaves. A flash of orange seen in a woodland becomes more vivid and the green of the trees appears more intense. However, proportion is important. The quieter color should be the prevailing one, the bright one a spot of contrast.

## Harmonious colors

Harmonious colors are those that sit next to each other on the color wheel, such as blue and purple, or yellow and orange. These do not contrast as complementary colors do,

but produce a more subtle effect. The most popular harmonious color schemes are pink, purple, and blue, or the hot colors of red, orange, and yellow.

If you want a very natural effect and a garden that will blend with the surrounding countryside, then you need to stick to pale, harmonious colors, particularly in spring. Trees and shrubs with green or white flowers fit wonderfully with the fresh green of new leaves, the white and pale yellow of the earliest bulbs, and herbaceous flowers. As the greens get darker later in the year, the brighter colors work well with them. If you are planning a city garden, green and white are cool and restful throughout the summer. On the other hand, enclosed gardens in built-up areas can be enclaves of vivid color and dramatic foliage, unrelated to their surroundings. The choice is yours.

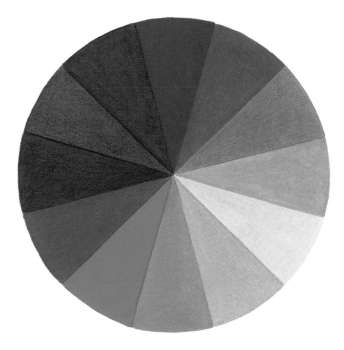

The color wheel shows how different colors relate to each other and can help in planning a color scheme.

## SINGLE-COLOR SCHEMES

Ever since Vita Sackville West devised her White Garden in Sissinghurst, England, single-color gardens have been popular. It is not difficult to create a one-color border, and the restriction in color keeps the planting from looking fussy and gives it a unity that is advantageous in a small garden.

# Choosing colors

WHETHER YOU WANT TO CREATE A SPECIFIC MOOD IN YOUR GARDEN or have a particular problem that you need to solve, color is one of the most important considerations. Below are lists of selected plants, ordered by color group, to give you some ideas as to the effect that different colors have and which plants you can use to get that splash of color.

## BLUE AND PURPLE

Blue flowers give a cooling effect and create a sense of distance. Finding true blue climbers, however, is not easy and most blues have a tinge of purple about them. Purple covers a wide range of colors, including mauves, lavenders, lilac, and violet. Purple and violet are rich, sumptuous colors with a fair amount of pink in them, while lavenders and lilac are cool and, like blue, have a distancing effect.

*Aconitum hemsleyanum*
*Clematis alpina* 'Francis Rivis'
*Clematis* 'Lasurstern'
*Clematis* 'Perle d'Azur'
*Cobaea scandens*
*Codonopsis convolvulacea*
*Ipomoea indica, I. tricolor*
*Lathyrus*

*Passiflora caerulea*
*Plumbago auriculata*
*Sollya heterophylla*
*Thunbergia grandiflora*
*Tropaeoleum azureum*
*Tweedia caerulea*
*Wisteria*

## RED AND PINK

Red flowers are always eye-catching; use them to draw attention to a particular feature or to distract from an ugly area. There are several good red roses, and in tropical regions there are some wonderful reds. Pink flowers have a pretty, old-fashioned effect, though different pinks vary hugely from deep purple-pinks to rich red-pinks and soft pastel pinks. If you are aiming for a cottage garden effect, try growing some pink, small-flowered climbers to create the desired effect.

*Actinidia kolomikta*
*Asteranthera ovata*
*Berberidopsis corallina*
*Clematis* 'Ernest Markham'
*Clematis* 'Niobe'
*C.* 'Nelly Moser'
*Clianthus puniceus*
*Distictis buccinatoria*
*Eccremocarpus scaber*
*Gloriosa superba*
*Ipomoea lobata*
*Ipomoea quamoclit*
*Jasminum beesianum*
*J. × stephanense*
*Lathyrus latifolius*
*L. odoratus*
*L. rotundifolius*
*Lonicera × brownii* 'Dropmore Scarlet'

*L. × italica*
*L. periclymenum* 'Serotina'
*Maurandya barclayana*
*M. erubescens*
*Metrosideros carmineus*
*Rhodochiton atrosanguineus*
*Rosa* (see pages 32–33 for examples)
*Tropaeolum majus* 'Crimson Beauty'
*T. m.* 'Crimson Velvet'
*T. m.* 'Darjeeling Red'
*T. m.* 'Empress of India'
*T. m.* 'Forest Flame'
*T. m.* 'Hermine Grashoff'
*Tropaeolum speciosum*

Left: The fascinating detail of *Passiflora caerulea*, the hardiest of the passionflowers.

Right: The vigorous white-flowered rambler rose, 'Rambling Rector,' is trained so that it looks like a spectacular weeping tree, impossible to overlook. The small flowers ensure that it fits well into this country garden.

## YELLOW AND ORANGE

Yellow is a warm color and brightens up a garden, especially in the winter. In cooler regions, yellow is a welcome sunny color. However, it can look brassy and garish and is often rather perversely "out of fashion." This also applies to orange, another warm color, useful for adding a tropical effect or bringing a border to life.

*Allamanda cathartica*
*Bomarea caldasii*
*Campsis*
*Clematis orientalis* 'Bill Mackenzie'
*C. tangutica*
*Eccremocarpus scaber*
*Jasminum nudiflorum*
*L. etrusca*
*L. e.* 'Donald Waterer'
*L. e.* 'Michael Rosse'
*L. e.* 'Superba'

*Lonicera* × *heckrottii*
*L.* × *heckrottii* 'Gold Flame'
*L. hildebrandiana*
*L. japonica* 'Halliana'
*L. sempervirens f. sulphurea*
*L.* × *tellmanniana*
*L. tragophylla*
*Thunbergia alata*
*Tropaeolum majus*
*T. peregrinum*
*T. tuberosum.* var. *lineamaculatum* 'Ken Aslet'

## WHITE AND CREAM

White flowers can light up corners in shady areas and they are useful for toning down some of the more brash colors. Some whites are more penetrating than others. Stephanotis, for example, is a very stark white, while the white wisteria can be pale pink or have a hint of lavender. Creams can vary from ivory to pale buttery yellows, and have a softer effect than pure white.

*Araujia sericifera*
*Clematis alpina* 'White Columbine'
*C. montana grandiflora*
*Clianthus puniceus* 'Albus'
*Codonopsis convolvulacea* 'Alba'
*Hydrangea anomala petiolaris*
*Jasminum officinale*
*J. o. affine*
*J. o.* 'Argenteovariegatum'

*J. polyanthum*
*Passiflora caerulea* 'Constance Elliott'
*Rosa* (see pages 32–33 for examples)
*Schizophragma hydrangeoides*
*S. integrifolium*
*Trachelospermum jasminoides*
*Wisteria brachybotrys*
*Wisteria sinensis* 'Alba'

# Greens

GREEN IS THE MOST PREVALENT COLOR IN THE GARDEN and comes in many shades and, just as importantly, many textures. Capability Brown and other landscape designers used the different greens of foliage alone to frame or hide a feature or to draw the eye onward.

The effect of leaf size on a plant or how it actually climbs changes the way the plant looks. Large leaves appear instantly exotic while small leaves and a scrambling habit are more in the style of cottage gardens: Think of honeysuckle or wild roses.

The surfaces of leaves vary as well, not only from plant to plant but from season to season. Ivy, an often-neglected plant, has bright glossy leaves in spring but later in the year the leaves darken and can seem dull and drab. If you want to get light in a corner, use climbers with glossy evergreen foliage that will shine and reflect every bit of light there is.

## HANDSOME LEAVES AND FALL TINTS

The *Parthenocissus* are wonderful foliage plants with large, shapely leaves that will densely cover a wall or fence. As an added bonus, they take on glorious fall colors in shades of orange, flame, and crimson before the leaves fall. The most common plants are the Boston ivy (*Parthenocissus tricuspidata*), the Chinese Virginia creeper (*P. henryana*), and the Virginia creeper (*P. quinquefolia*). These are all self-clinging climbers.

*Parthenocissus quinquefolia*, the well-known Virginia creeper, has fresh green new leaves in spring, which turn into rich shades of orange-red in the fall.

## IVY

Ivy is perhaps the most underrated of climbing plants. Its very ubiquity, its hardiness and ease of cultivation, and its reputation for destroying walls means that this handsome and worthwhile plant is often ignored when climbers are being considered. Yet it has a number of uses, and when it is used and grown well, it can be quite attractive.

Sound walls, whether brick, stone, or stucco, will not be damaged by ivy. Most small gardens, enclosed patios, or yards could benefit from the rich, permanent green of ivy leaves. In the early part of the year the fresh, glossy green of their new leaves is as heartening as any spring flower.

Ivy can be used to outline an arch, create a false pillar, or completely cover an area. Retaining walls built of breeze blocks can be disguised with ivy. It can be combined with other climbing plants like *Clematis armandii* or the annual (in temperate zones) *Eccremocarpus scaber* for color, or you can have a group of mixed ivies. *Hedera helix* 'Oro di Bogliasco' is colorful, with yellow-centered leaves and pink stems. Avoid the plain native *Hedera helix*, which can eventually become invasive. Choose instead one of the many distinctive varieties that are much less rampant.

*Hedera colchica* is believed by many to be the finest of all ivies. The leaves can be 8 in. long and it is a strong grower. The variegated forms *H. colchica* 'Dentata Variegata' and *Hedera colchica* 'Sulphur Heart' ('Paddy's Pride') are especially eye-catching. The Irish ivy *H. hibernica* has broad leaves and is another good grower.

## FOLIAGE FOR SHELTERED SPOTS

Other evergreens for year-round effect include the slightly tender *Trachelospermum jasminoides* and *T. asiaticum*. They both need the protection of warm walls to flourish. They have fragrant white flowers in clusters at the ends of their shoots and need to be tied to supports. Although grown for their flowers, the leaves are particularly good. *Stauntonia hexaphylla*, with dark, glossy leaves and small clusters of white, fragrant flowers in spring, is another example of a slightly tender plant that is well worth trying. In a good year, it even produces purple-red fruits. *Solanum crispum* 'Glasnevin' is semievergreen in mild winters, as is its cousin, the not quite as hardy *Solanum jasminoides* 'Album'. These are both really grown for their flowers but the foliage is a bonus. 'Glasnevin' has clusters of showy blue-purple potato flowers, while those of *S. j.* 'Album' are white.

*Pileostegia viburnoides*, a member of the hydrangea family, is evergreen and quite hardy. It needs a warm wall to flower well but is known to thrive on a sheltered north wall. The handsome leaves are narrow and corrugated. The flowers are small and white, in flattish panicles.

## FOLIAGE AND FLOWERS

The evergreen Japanese honeysuckles, *Lonicera japonica* 'Halliana' and *L. henryi*, are, like ivies, underrated and underused plants. *L. j.* 'Aureoreticulata' was popular at one time for its variegated leaves, green netted with yellow, but its flowers are inconspicuous. *L. j.* 'Halliana' is quick growing and vigorous, and the florets in the leaf joints, which are white fading to yellow, are highly scented and produced over a long period in summer. It will grow almost anywhere and will soon cover a tree, pergola, or trellis. *L. etrusca* 'Superba' has bolder flowers in creamy yellow but it is slightly tender and needs a warm spot.

## MAKING PATTERNS WITH EVERGREENS

Many evergreen climbers can be trained so that they form patterns on a wall, rather than covering the whole wall. Plants such as ivy, *Euonymus fortunei radicans*, *Ficus pumila*, and *Periploca graeca* can be trained into squares, diamonds, or even free-forms against plain walls. This idea is especially suitable on an attractive wall that you do not want to cover entirely with foliage. It is very easy to do by pinching out shoots and new growth that are not going where you want them to.

Ivies (*Hedera* sp. and cvs) can be easily trained to create dramatic effects. Here the ivy is grown to form a crisscross pattern, which breaks up, but does not conceal, a length of brick wall. To make this pattern, use two plants in each planting hole, training one diagonally to the left and the other to the right. Ivy needs to be supported for the first year until it puts out aerial roots.

# Using roses for their color

FOR MOST PEOPLE, ROSES ARE IN A LEAGUE OF THEIR OWN when it comes to color. They are the most popular climbers, grown for their scent and superb flowers in shades of deep purple through red to pink and white, and from white to cream, yellow, orange, vermilion, and almost brown. They are midsummer flowers and the often-intense colors balance with the deeper green of summer leaves.

## SOME RECOMMENDATIONS

• To make the bottom of the garden seem further away, choose *Rosa* 'Veilchenblau', which is the bluest of climbing roses, or pale pinks and soft yellows.

• If the views from the garden are not good, choose dramatic roses that will attract attention inside the garden. Large white roses like *R.* 'Climbing Iceberg' jump forward and are ideal for distracting the eye from an ugly building.

• A pergola or line of pillars clad with bright red or yellow roses will also draw the eye and create a striking feature.

• If you want roses that are pale and cool, choose 'Albéric Barbier', which is yellow in bud and opens to a creamy white, or 'New Dawn', which is a pale flesh pink and seems to go with everything except other "blue" pinks.

• Sumptuous dark-red roses, such as *R.* 'Guinée', a climbing hybrid tea with a delicious scent, are perfect for romantic plantings and they need to be seen close up. Beware, however: 'Guinée' is difficult to grow and can be rough with its flowers. 'Climbing Etoile d'Hollande', another rich red rose, is easier but its brilliance does not have quite the same romantic appeal.

*Rosa* 'Climbing Iceberg' grabs attention with its clusters of large white flowers over a long season.

**RED**
'Altissimo'
'Château de Clos-Vougeot'
'Climbing Crimson Glory'
'Macdub' (Dublin Bay)
'Parkdirektor Riggers'
'Paul's Scarlet Climber'
'Tess of the D'Urbervilles'

**WHITE and CREAM**
'Albéric Barbier'
'Félicité Perpétue'
*R. filipes* 'Kiftsgate'
'Madame Alfred Carrière'
'Rambling Rector'
'Wedding Day'
'White Cockade'

**YELLOW**
'Céline Forestier'
'Clarence House'
'Emily Gray'
'Gloire de Dijon'
'Golden Showers'
'Graham Thomas'
'Leverkusen'
'Maigold'
'Mermaid'

**ORANGE**
'Climbing Bettina'
'Crown Princess Margareta'
*R. foetida* 'Bicolor'
'Harquanne' (Breath of Life)
'Joseph's Coat'
'President Herbert Hoover'
'Schoolgirl'

**PINK**
'Albertine'
'Aloha'
'Baltimore Belle'
'Bantry Bay'
'Blairii No. 2.'
'Chaplin's Pink'
'Constance Spry'
'Madame Grégoire Staechelin'
'New Dawn'
'Zéphirine Drouhin'

**PURPLE**
'Archiduc Joseph'
'Bleu Magenta'
'Rose-Marie Viaud'
'Veilchenblau'
'William Lobb'

# A colonnade of color

A colonnade is a useful way of dividing a garden visually and giving some height without losing light or a feeling of space. It is basically a series of columns linked together, over which climbing plants can be trained. Rambling roses are particularly suited to this type of structure. Architectural colonnades are seen in formal rose gardens, with brick columns and wooden crosspieces. A wooden colonnade linked with rope will do the same thing more cheaply and makes a handsome garden feature.

To make this structure you will need pressure-treated wooden uprights at least 6 x 6 in. square or very sturdy rustic wood poles at least 6 in. in diameter. They need to be about 10 ft. in length. You will also need bulky rope, about 2 in. in diameter, to link the uprights. Decide how far apart you want your uprights to be, calculate how much rope you need, and add sufficient length to make a good knot on each end of the rope.

1 Drill holes through each upright large enough to thread the rope through, about 3 in. from the top.

2 Arrange the uprights 7–10 ft. apart and, making sure the drilled holes are aligned, set them in holes about 20 in. deep and 12 in. square (A). Pack rubble around the base of each upright and prop them up straight with temporary battens. Tamp a concrete mix hard around them and leave to set.

3 Thread the rope through the holes in the uprights so that it hangs down a little, creating an attractive scalloped effect. When doing this, bear in mind that the rope will probably lengthen a little over time. Knot firmly in place (B).

4 Cover the uprights with a capping of lead, galvanized metal, or a wooden finial to keep rain from seeping in.

## PLANTING THE ROSES

When making planting holes, position them so that the prevailing wind will blow the plants toward the uprights rather than away (see pages 10–11 for more details on planting). Twist the roses around the uprights, as this encourages the production of flowering shoots. Rose stems need to be trained into a suitable position while they are still young and pliant. Tie them to the uprights with plastic rose ties, string, or raffia.

## CHOOSING ROSES

Rambling roses are best suited to growing over a colonnade. Choose from the following:

'Alexander Girault'
'François Juranville'
'Ghislaine de Féligonde'
'New Dawn'
'Phyllis Bide'
'Tour de Malakoff'
'Veilchenblau'
'William Lobb'

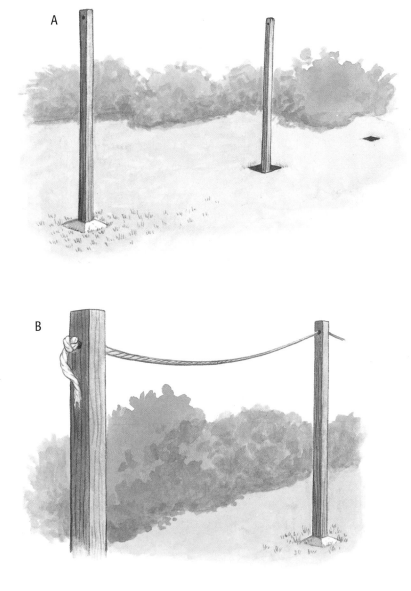

A

B

# Color through the year

IT IS EASY TO HAVE A COLORFUL GARDEN IN SUMMER–too easy sometimes, for the garden can be full of summer-flowering climbers with no room for climbers that are interesting at other times. To extend the interest through into fall, winter, and early spring takes more planning, particularly if there is a color theme to the garden.

## Evergreen Climbers for Temperate and Warm Temperate Regions

• *Asteranthera ovata*, a clinging climber with small leaves in opposite pairs and glowing red tubular flowers.

• *Berberidopsis corallina* has leathery green leaves and hanging clusters of rich red globular flowers.

• *Clematis armandii* has large, elliptical leaves and clusters of small, white, scented flowers in late winter and early spring.

• *Clematis cirrhosa*, *C. c.* var. *balearica* and *C. c.* 'Freckles' have attractive fern-like foliage and small, creamy-white, bell-shaped flowers. The two variants are spotted inside, 'Freckles' being the most vivid.

• *Euonymus fortunei*, often seen as a shrub with glossy, deep green leaves, but it will produce roots on the stems, as ivy does, when it has reached the top of its support. There are small orange seeds in pinkish cases in the fall.

• *Hedera*, a self-clinging climber with several important species and hundreds of cultivars.

• *Pileostegia viburnoides*, a root climber with long, oval leaves and flattened heads of creamy white flowers in the fall.

• *Stauntonia hexaphylla* has dark, glossy leaves and small clusters of white, fragrant flowers in early spring. In a good year it even produces purple-red fruits.

The large leaves of *Hedera colchica dentata* 'Variegata,' the Persian Ivy, are bright and cheerful all year round.

• *Trachelospermum* has glossy green leaves in opposite pairs. *T. asiaticum* is shy flowering, with jasmine-like white flowers fading to yellow. *T. jasminoides* has larger, very fragrant flowers but is not so hardy.

## Spring

• *Akebia quinata* is a vigorous twining climber with pale green leaves and unusual, chocolate-purple flowers.

• *Clematis alpina* is a slender climber with pendulous, lantern-shaped flowers in blue, white, or pink.

• *Clematis macropetala*–as the name indicates, the bell-shaped blue, pink, or white flowers on these species are semidouble, the centers full of small, narrow petals.

• *Clematis montana*–white or pink four-petaled flowers smother this very vigorous plant in late spring and early summer every year.

• *Rosa banksiae* 'Lutea'–an almost-thornless rose with small, double, pale yellow flowers in hanging clusters.

## Summer

• *Clematis* sp. (large-flowered), summer-flowering hybrids with flowers that can be 8 in. across. They are usually in shades of white, pink, lavender, purple, and deep red.

• *Jasminum* sp., a family containing well-known climbers such as *Jasminum officinale*, the common white jasmine, a twiner bearing pure white, scented flowers in clusters from midsummer to midfall. *J. polyanthum*, with pink buds, is not so hardy.

• *Lathyrus odoratus*–Sweet peas are hardy annuals that climb using leaf tendrils. There are many different colors and they are easy to grow from seeds.

• *Lonicera* sp.–climbing honeysuckle species and cultivars have long tubular flowers in pairs, sometimes borne singly, as in the Japanese honeysuckle, and sometimes in clusters, as in the native honeysuckle *L. periclymenum* and *L. p.* 'Belgica,' with red and yellow flowers.

• *Rosa* sp.–summer is the best time for climbing and rambling roses of all colors, from bluish lilac to white, cream, yellow, and red.

## Fall

- *Ampelopsis glandulosa brevipedunculata*, a vigorous vine with bright blue berries. *A. g. b.* 'Elegans' has white variegated leaves.
- *Celastrus orbiculatus*, a twiner with red seeds in yellow-lined seed cases in the fall.
- *Clematis sp.*–there are three climbing clematis species that flower from late summer on into the fall. They are *C. orientalis*, *C. rehderiana*, and *C. tangutica*. They all have small yellow flowers. *C. viticella* cultivars, like 'Purpurea Plena Elegans' and 'Etoile Violette', will flower until early fall.
- *Solanum crispum* 'Album' has white potato flowers and green leaves, and flourishes until the frosts.
- *Tropaeolum speciosum*–scarlet flowers in summer, purple bracts and blue berries in the fall.
- *Vitis coignetiae*, a vigorous ornamental vine with large rounded leaves, green on top and covered with reddish hairs underneath. In the fall the leaves turn rich apricot to red.

## GARDEN KNOW-HOW

# Training a colorful climber around a pillar

Create a wonderful feature in the garden by growing two beautiful climbing roses around a pillar. You may be lucky enough to find a stone pillar in a salvage yard or have a tree with a straight, bare trunk. If not, a piece of wood about 8 in. in diameter and between 6–9 ft. long can be set firmly in concrete in the ground or a very simple brick column can be constructed.

1 Select two young climbing roses, ensuring that the main stems are very pliable. Make a planting hole on either side of the pillar and plant the roses (A). See page 33 for more guidance on how to plant a rose.

2 Guide the leaders of one rose to go clockwise and the other to go counterclockwise so that the stems cross over, making a pattern of squares over the pillar (B). Fix in position on a wooden pillar using lead-headed nails or, if the pillars are stone or brick, use proprietary plastic ties with discs that stick firmly to any surface (C).

3 Training the stems so that they are more horizontal than vertical encourages the branches to produce flowering laterals all along their length rather than just at the top (D).

4 Remove unwanted main stems unless you want only one type of rose on your pillar (E). The rose will have more than one stem and it is quite possible to train them in opposite directions to get the same lattice effect as when using two plants. When the main stem has reached the top of the pillar, pinch the top back (F).

5 Each year, after flowering, cut back the laterals to two or three outward-facing buds. Mulch the base with well-rotted manure in winter (G).

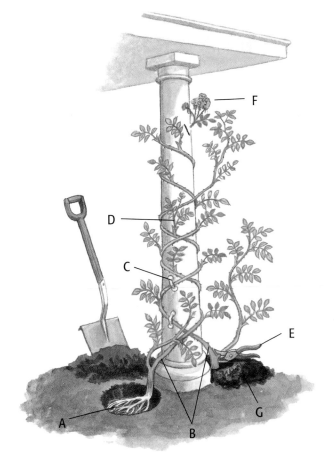

### CHOOSING PLANTS

Do not choose roses that are too vigorous. *R.* 'Zephirine Drouhin,' *R.* 'White Cockade,' *R.* 'Little Rambler,' *R.* 'Phyllis Bide,' or *R.* 'Paul's Scarlet Climber' are good choices.

Pairs of clematises look very effective when grown this way, but the pillar would need to be covered with netting for the clematises to attach themselves to. Most hybrid clematises would be suitable (for suggestions, see page 66).

To extend the season of interest of a rose-covered pillar, add an early flowering clematis such as *C. alpina* 'White Columbine,' *C. a.* 'Francis Rivis' (which is blue), fluffy blue *C. macropetala*, or *C. m.* 'Markham's Pink,' and even a late flowering viticella hybrid such as *C. texensis* 'Duchess of Wales.' The rose stems will provide good support for the clematises.

# DESIGNING WITH CLIMBERS

*F*or most of us, garden design seems to be a rather frightening subject, best left to the experts. Much design, however, is simply problem solving, particularly in a modestly sized garden. What to hide, what to draw attention to, how to add height to a flat site, how to manage the difference between levels—these are all problems that can be solved by using climbing plants on different supports. When planning a garden layout, scale and proportion are important. There should be a pleasing relationship between the length, width, and height of features and their relationship to the elements around them. Even in a small, enclosed garden you need to think on a larger scale than at first seems necessary. Features are more often too small rather than too big. To get the scale right, use bamboo canes or scrap wood to represent the new features you are planning and try them in the garden for size and position. Designers learn to visualize the scale of things or they draw scale plans, but most of us need to see something in place before we know what it will look like when it is done.

Rose-covered arches frame a pretty fountain silhouetted against a background of sober yew. The series of arches is planted with *Rosa* 'Seagull' and are sufficiently far apart to allow plenty of light through, enabling *Nepeta* 'Six Hills Giant' to flourish.

# Arches and arbors

ARCHES CAN BE USED AS EYE-CATCHERS, but they work better if they are positioned to frame a view, a path, or a small feature, which can be as modest as a pot of summer bedding. An arbor is a shaded bower, usually a wooden or metal structure clothed in climbing plants, that offers a private place to sit and relax.

## ARCHES

Simple frame arches covered in climbers are a quick way of bringing height into a garden; this avoids the dense shade that a tree of the same height would give and you can plant close to the uprights. An arch will also determine how people look at space. If you want people to look down your path or at a sculpture, frame the approach with an arch.

You need to be able to stand well back from an arch to look through it properly, so in a small garden place the arch at the far end of the garden, over a sundial, birdbath, or other ornament.

In a city garden, an arch should be architectural in style, perhaps with a trellis to support climbers. Avoid rustic arches, which look better in a country garden or well away from the house. The city garden arch needs to look attractive by itself, but not too flamboyant or it will detract from the climbing plants that clothe it.

## Framing a view

When framing an attractive view, use less-elaborate climbers, which are plain when seen up close, but at a distance do not distract from the scene they are meant to frame.
• *Celastrus orbicularis* has bright fruits and leaves in the fall, at a time of the year when you might like to draw the interest inside the garden because the leaves have fallen from trees outside your boundary, revealing surroundings that are a little humdrum.
• *Clematis rehderiana* has small, pale yellow, bell-shaped flowers in clusters, and should be cut down in early spring to about 12 in. from the ground.
• *Humulus lupulus* and *H. l.* 'Aurea' are two fast-growing, herbaceous perennials that twine. The lobed, maplelike leaves are rough to the touch.
• *Solanum jasminoides* 'Album' has small leaves and delicate white potato flowers in late summer. It needs to be cut back every winter except in milder areas, but is vigorous and soon makes up for lost time.

Brick gateposts and an iron frame make a sound structure for the vigorous and floriferous clematis, *C. Jackmanii*.

### CHOOSING PLANTS FOR ARCHES
As the arch is a frame to a "picture," it is more effective if it is planted either with dark leaves or with bright flowers that appear to jump forward. It should draw first the eye and then the footsteps toward it. From the north facade of a house, an arch covered with ivy or other dark evergreen will make the sunny area beyond look even more tempting. Plant the area beyond with receding colors and gray-leaved plants. On the south side of a house, looking toward the end of the garden, which will be the shady north side of the boundary fence or wall, plant the arch with strong, bright colors that jump forward and the garden through the arch with quieter colors to make the distance beyond the arch seem longer.

# Making a temporary arbor

Create a temporary arbor with planting boxes and trellis supports. If you have just moved into a house and are not yet sure what you want to do with the garden or perhaps are just renting, you can make a temporary arbor to shelter a garden bench using readily available materials and quick-growing annual climbers. Choose a site that gets sun in the morning or late afternoon.

**1** Choose two square planting boxes, 12 x 12 in. or bigger, and trellis panels, slightly narrower, that are made with two extensions at the bottom. Most garden centers will stock these.

**2** Put stones or broken pots into the bottoms of the boxes and support the trellis with them.

**3** Put the boxes in place before you fill them up with good-quality, soil-based potting compost (A). Add slow-release fertilizer, following the manufacturer's instructions.

**4** Plant annuals or climbers like sweet peas, black-eyed Susan, morning glories, *Rhodochiton atrosanguineus*, or canary creeper to climb over the trellis (see pages 56–57). Complete the planting by adding scented bedding plants such as heliotrope to the boxes (B).

**5** Link the two side pieces with a piece of trellis, the same width as the side pieces, across the top (C) and, if you choose, another broader piece of trellis across the back. Wire the pieces together securely.

## PLANTS FOR ARBORS

Scented plants are the best choice if you intend to sit and relax under the arbor—choose exotic white jasmine, roses, or honeysuckle. The planting should not be too dense, as the arbor should be inviting rather than dark and spidery. Arbors can also be formed from plants alone, by shaping and training trees or shrubs such as yew.

If you want something discreet, try *Ampelopsis megalophylla*, which has long leaves and will create a very private place, or the evergreen *Holboellia coriacea*, which is strongly scented. It has shiny leaves and two sorts of flowers that appear at the same time: The male flowers are purple-green bells in clusters, while the female flowers are larger and greenish-white with a purple tinge. Although the plant will survive temperatures of 50°F, it is best to mulch the plant well in winter if the arbor is not in a very sheltered position.

# Arcades and pergolas

AN ARCADE IS A SERIES OF ARCHES. Like a colonnade or series of columns, it can look confused if not well planted. Pergolas are very similar to arcades, but while an arcade has a curved top, the top of a pergola is always flat. There must be a strict relationship between width, height, and spacing for these features to look balanced.

## SITING A PERGOLA

Pergolas and arcades are large features and may be too big for a small garden, particularly if erected down the middle. At first a pergola seems to add height, but it also creates a strong horizontal axis with the repetition of the columns. In a large garden, a pergola can make a wonderful feature, providing a support for many climbing plants.

Like a colonnade, a pergola can make a useful division if built across the garden. It can also be erected against the back or sides of a house or the side walls or fences of a garden so as to create a cloister effect. If the pergola is to be built near the house, it looks better if it is more architectural and the materials are related to those of the house with, for example, brick columns in the same type of brick as that of the house. If possible, lay a paved or gravel path underneath a pergola, as little will flourish in the deep shade.

Remember that a pergola, like an arch, works as a picture frame and it should always lead to something, perhaps a garden seat or an urn of flowers.

Climbers can be planted quite close to the uprights of a pergola. Unlike trees or walls, the soil at the base of a pergola is unlikely to be particularly dry.

A charming rustic pergola supports a variety of pink and red roses.

## CLIMBERS FOR PERGOLAS

A large pergola can support some magnificent plants. Apart from some of the larger roses, the classic pergola plant is a wisteria. For a few weeks each year the long racemes of mauve or white fragrant flowers hang down inside the pergola, creating a magical cave.
Other good plants to consider are:
• *Actinidia kolomikta* has green leaves with attractive pink and white tips.
• *Akebia quinata* has unusual brownish–purple flowers that have a vanilla scent in spring.
• *Clematis sp.*—almost any clematis can be paired with other climbers on a sturdy pergola as well.
• *Humulus lupulus* 'Aureus', the golden hop.

• *Jasminum officinale* has feathery green leaves and small, white, heavily-scented flowers, luxuriantly borne.
• *Lonicera × heckrottii* has showy panicles of yellow flowers with red buds.
• *Passiflora caerulea* 'Constance Elliot', the lovely white passionflower, which is perfect for a pergola in a warm area.
• *Periploca graeca*, the silk vine is a strong grower and has dark, shiny foliage. The brownish–purple flowers are interesting but smell unpleasant and are followed by pods containing seeds, each of which has a long tuft of silky hairs.
• *Schisandra rubriflora*, with brilliantly colored red flowers.
• *Solanum crispum* 'Glasnevin', with purple potato flowers.
• *Vitis coignetiae*, the crimson glory vine; it has wonderful fall coloring.

# Building a pergola

A pergola built against a house wall is easier and cheaper to make than a freestanding feature and creates a simple cloister effect. Three uprights are the minimum number for a small pergola and they should be placed about 6 ft. apart at their centers. Crosspieces join the uprights to the wall opposite where they are fixed to a wooden house plate. The uprights should be placed no further than 8 ft. from the side of the house. The uprights should be made of 4 x 4 in. pressure-treated wood, 10 ft. long. You will need six crosspieces made of 4 x 1 in. wood, 10 ft. long. The house plate should be made of 4 x 2 in. wood, approximately 12 ft. long. You will also need a piece of wood to act as a brace, 4 x 1 in., approximately 12 ft. long.

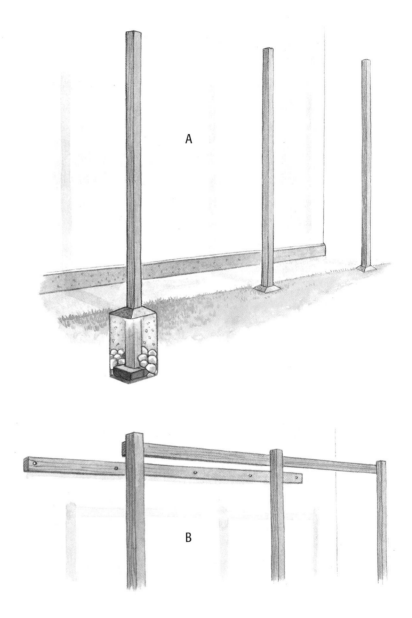

1 Dig a hole for each upright, 12 in. square and 24 in. deep. Put two engineering bricks in the bottom of the hole and then put the posts in. Pack some hardcore or stones around the bases of the posts to hold them in place. Make sure they are vertical, level, and in alignment with each other and support with temporary battens. Tamp a concrete mix hard around the uprights, beveling the top of the concrete so that it slopes away from the post in all directions. Leave to set (A).

2 Fix the wooden plate to the house wall, making sure the top of the plate is at exactly the same height as the top of the uprights. Drill through the wood into the house wall and secure firmly in place with bolts (B).

3 Cut the wood brace to fit the total width of the structure and fix it to all three uprights on the inside of the structure, about 2 in. down from the top, using bolts. This will hold the pergola square.

4 Cut the six crosspieces to length, so that they will extend just beyond the uprights. You may also like to jigsaw a curve into one end of each crosspiece to create an attractive finish. Cut a 2-in.-deep notch on four of the crosspieces at the point where they will slot over the brace. Use bolts or nails to fix each crosspiece firmly in place on either side of each upright. Drive nails in at an angle to fix the end of each crosspiece to the wall plate, or use galvanized fixings (C).

**TRAINING ROSES**
Remember, if you are using climbing roses on your pergola, twist the main shoots around the uprights, fixing them with plastic rose ties or string while they are still pliable. Cut any side shoots back to three or four buds each spring to encourage flowering and to keep the roses under control.

# Focal points

CLIMBING PLANTS CAN BE USED IN many different ways to create focal points, some more permanent than others. Obelisks and pillars constructed from wood or trellis make good semipermanent features in a garden. They can be planted with permanent plants such as roses or honeysuckle, or with more transient plants such as *Lathyrus grandiflorus*. Climbers trained as standards can be either a fixed or temporary feature depending upon where they are planted, and ivy topiary in a pot is a simple way to create a feature that can be moved around in the garden.

## PLANTS FOR OBELISKS

• *Thladiantha dubia* is from the same family as the cucumber and has yellow flowers and heart-shaped leaves.
• Also good in this kind of situation are the maurandyas and lophospermums, twining snapdragons. *Lophospermum*

*erubescens* (syn. *Asarina erubescens*) and *Maurandya barclayana* can be grown from seed, but need well-drained soil and a sheltered spot. These are sometimes referred to as "asarina" in seed catalogs.
• *Codonopsis convolvulacea*, with lilac, five-petaled flowers, needs dappled shade.

## GARDEN KNOW-HOW

## Ivy topiary

Ivy can be used to make topiary focal points. It can be grown around a wire frame inserted into a large pot. These frames are usually painted dark green, come in a variety of shapes and sizes, and are readily available. Alternatively, you can make a simple shape from chicken wire, stuffed with moss.

1 Insert the legs of the frame or the wire construction into a container filled with good compost. Make sure the container is not too flimsy.

2 Plant an ivy plant by each upright and pack it in, adding more compost if necessary. Water well (A).

3 You will need to tie the ivy stems to the uprights until they begin to mesh together. Pinch out stems that are too wayward (B).

4 When the frame has been completely covered by the ivy, maintain the shape by trimming the ivy with a pair of shears.

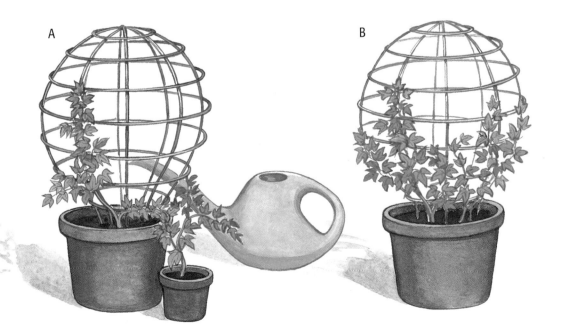

A

B

## How to make a standard wisteria

Standard roses, where flowers and leaves develop from a straight, bare stem up to 6 ft. high, are quite common. Many other plants can be trained in this way, including wisteria. Standards are useful because in full bloom they make an eye-catching feature while allowing other plants to be grown right beneath them. The Chinese wisteria, *W. sinensis*, or one of its cultivars, is the species to grow because of the spectacularly long racemes of flowers.

1 Plant your wisteria, either in a 15-in. pot of John Innes No. 3 compost, or in the ground in a prepared planting hole (see page 10). Support the main stem with a sturdy cane (A). Water well.

2 Remove any other shoots. When the main stem has grown to 20 in. beyond the top of the support, remove the tip.

3 Lateral shoots should then appear along the whole length of the stem. Shorten these side shoots back to four or five leaves (B), but let the shoots at the top grow to the length you want. These will form the "umbrella" at the top of the stem. Leaving a few leaves on the stem strengthens it.

4 After about two years, when the upper branch system—the ribs of the umbrella—is well developed, you can remove all the short branches on the lower part of the stem. The wisteria will need to be kept staked (C).

A      B      C

### OTHER CLIMBERS TO BE TRAINED AS STANDARDS:

| | |
|---|---|
| *Bougainvillea* | *Petrea volubilis* |
| *Jasminum azoricum* | *Stephanotis floribunda* |
| *Lonicera japonica* | *Trachelospermum* |
| *Mandevilla splendens* | *jasminoides* |

### STANDARD ROSES

The following climbing roses make excellent standards:

| | |
|---|---|
| 'Albéric Barbier' | 'Félicité Perpetué' |
| 'Albertine' | 'Francois Juranville' |
| 'Dorothy Perkins' | 'Golden Glow' |
| 'Excelsa' | 'Minnehaha' |
| 'Emily Grey' | 'Sanders White' |

# Temporary eye-catchers

EVEN IN THE SMALLEST GARDEN, you can create temporary focal points by using pots containing a wigwam of canes supporting exotic tender climbers. Group them on the patio in the summer or drop them in to fill gaps in beds and borders, where they will add instant height and color.

There are lots of very showy, tender climbers that will bring an exotic feel to the garden. If you don't have anywhere to protect them from frost in the winter months, such as a greenhouse, then choose annual climbers instead, which will flower profusely through the summer and die off in the fall, such as sweet peas and black–eyed Susan.

You can use these temporary features either singly or in groups, creating a rhythm in the garden border. Placed symmetrically in twos and fours, they give a very formal effect, while in threes the effect is more relaxed.

## PLANTS TO CHOOSE

- Sweet peas (*Lathyrus odoratus*) are well-known annuals that provide summer color and perfume.
- *Ipomoea quamoclit* is an annual morning glory with bright crimson flowers.
- The quick-growing black-eyed Susan (*Thunbergia alata*) is an annual with vivid orange flowers and a black eye.
- *Passiflora* 'Allardi' is a perennial with blue, pink, and white flowers and is scented.
- *Senecio macroglossus* 'Variegatus' has variegated ivy-shaped leaves and white daisy flowers. It is also a perennial.
- *Sollya heterophylla*, the Australian bluebell, is a perennial with pale green lanceolate leaves and sky-blue, bell-shaped flowers, ½ in. long.
- *Ipomoea indica*, the evergreen, perennial morning glory has rich purple-blue flowers, aging to reddish-pink.
- *Chorizema cordatum*, the Australian flame pea, has bunches of small pea flowers in orange with a purple keel. It is a perennial.

The annual climber, black-eyed Susan, *Thunbergia alata*, is ideal for growing up the simple supports, such as bamboo canes, to make a temporary focal point. Black-eyed Susan is widely available in shades of apricot, ivory, and yellow but seed mixtures can now be bought that produce a good proportion of red blooms.

This wicker structure has a modern shape but fits in well with these informal surroundings. Here it is forming a support for sweet peas, but later in the summer the nasturtiums rampaging around its base could easily take over. Many annual climbers prefer a rough-textured support, such as these twisted twigs, to smooth plastic, bamboo, or iron.

## MAKING A TEMPORARY SUPPORT

• To make a temporary support for short–lived or tender climbers, even one post driven into the ground will do.

• Other very simple structures to make or buy are bamboo or woven willow wigwams or obelisks. These bring a rustic feel to the garden, but the shapes are graphic enough to look at home in most situations.

• Architectural supports, such as obelisks, pillars, or columns, are also suitable.

• Try pyramids of softwood or painted or stained trellis.

• Metal supports are attractive. They are usually wrought iron, but these days even aluminum or galvanized zinc are often used.

• Perspex makes a very modern support for climbers but can only be obtained from some garden designers.

# PRACTICAL SOLUTIONS

*S*ome climbing plants are very good at concealing things. These are not necessarily the most eye-catching of climbers but they have the advantages of good, dense foliage and many are quick growing. Often, in a garden, covering an unattractive but immovable feature or blocking out ugly surroundings is as important as putting something beautiful in it. Climbers do a splendid job of growing up, over, or even along the ground, adding texture, color, and interest.

A well-established covering of *Wisteria sinensis* and *Lonicera* x *americana* turns a sober brick wall into a beautiful garden feature.

# Screens

CLIMBING PLANTS ARE IDEAL FOR SCREENING. Outdoor screens can be as varied as those found indoors. They can be either dense, completely concealing something, or fine like a veil. Whatever type of screen you want to create, climbing plants are preferable to the frequently chosen Leyland's cypress (× *Cupressocyparis leylandii*). There is, of course, the equivalent of a Leyland's cypress among the climbing plants and that is *Fallopia baldschuanica*, the Russian vine or "mile-a-minute" plant. On the whole, these rampant plants should be avoided in the garden–there are other tough plants in the climbing world that can be as effective but on a much smaller scale.

## QUICK ANNUAL SCREENS

There are many lovely fast-growing plants that will create colorful screens for the summer months. Many of the plants sold as annual climbers are, in fact, perennials that come from warm climates. They grow so fast and flower in the first year, so they can be used as annuals in cooler places. Treat them like any other tender bedding plant and put them in position when all danger of frost has passed in your area.

Most annual climbers are fairly insubstantial plants. To make a dense screen, plant them very thickly in well-prepared soil. Enriching the soil too much, however, tends to make the plant produce too many leaves at the expense of flowers, but this may be an advantage in some situations.

## CHOOSING ANNUAL AND HERBACEOUS CLIMBERS

• The cup and saucer vine (*Cobaea scandens*) is a very fast-growing perennial with large, intriguing flowers. The bell flowers could be described as a murky purple and there is also a pale green form, sold as 'Alba.' If cobaea is grown as an annual it should be started off early. Seeds can be tricky to germinate because they really need to be sown fresh. Sow the seeds on their edge singly in 3-in. pots. They will need potting on and pinching out, and then staking in cooler climates before it is time to put them out in the garden.
• The canary creeper (*Tropaeolum peregrinum*) grows to about 5 ft. and has small, yellow-fringed flowers. The effect is rather informal and the flowers do not have a great impact from a distance, but the screening quality is good. The leaves are prettily shaped like those of a fig. To ensure a long season of flower and leaf, buy two packets of seeds and sow one batch indoors in midwinter and the other packet outdoors at the end of spring when the soil has warmed up. Watch out for blackflies and cabbage white caterpillars.

• The Chilean glory flower (*Eccremocarpus scaber*) has orange-red tubular flowers. There are other colors available, including red (*E. s. carmineus*), yellow (*E. s. aureus*), and pink (*E. s. roseus*). This plant climbs using lots of tiny tendrils. In cold areas, it is killed in the winter, but in warmer regions it survives in the ground, even if cut back by frost. In very warm areas it flowers all year.
• *Rhodochiton atrosanguineus* has long, tubular, dark purple flowers with a pagoda top in reddish-purple and always attracts attention. It can grow to 5 ft. but is suitable for veiling rather than screening. Sow the seeds under glass in early spring.
• The kudzu vine (*Pueraria montana lobata*) grows from tuberous roots and will grow up to 30 ft. in a season. It makes a good screen or cover for buildings. It needs a hot wall to flower well, however. The flowers are purple and grow in bunches.

## SWEET PEA SCREENS

The best-known annual climber is the sweet pea (*Lathyrus odoratus*). People have been hybridizing sweet peas since about 1865 and there have been hundreds of varieties, although not all have lasted to the present day. As the flowers have become larger and the color range wider, so the perfume for which the sweet pea is so loved has become fainter, so be sure to choose a scented variety. The recently reintroduced 'Matucana,' which was one of the earliest varieties, has small, bicolored purple and reddish purple flowers and a particularly strong scent.

You can sow sweet peas, as you would edible beans and peas, along rows of bamboo canes to make a freestanding screen. This would be a good, yet easy and cheap way of screening off a vegetable plot. Alternatively, grow them up the plastic netting that is sold as pea and bean netting, attached to a fence or trellis.

This heavenly blue *Ipomoea sp.*, or morning glory, will twine happily around anything.

## GARDEN KNOW-HOW

## Success with sweet peas

Much of the mystique about growing sweet peas is aimed at enthusiasts who grow them for exhibition. Growing sweet peas to make a screen is quite simple.

1 Sow the seeds in late winter or early spring singly in 3-in. pots in seed compost (A). Some experts advise filing down the seed coats until the white of the seed shows through to help them germinate. Older varieties do not always need this.

2 Put the pots in a warm place or, if possible, in an electric propagator at 59°F. Remove from the propagator as soon as the seeds have germinated and place in a cold frame or other light, frost-free but unheated place.

3 When the plants are about 3 in. high, pinch out the tops to make the plants bushier. Plant out fall-sown plants in midspring and spring-sown plants in late spring, spacing them about 10–12 in. apart (B). The further apart the plants, the better the flowers. The soil should be moisture-retentive and have plenty of well-rotted manure or compost added to it. Sweet peas will happily stand partial shade.

4 Sweet peas will provide plenty of flowers, but they should be removed when they begin to fade. The formation of seed pods must be prevented if the plant is to continue flowering. If this is done you should get flowers for at least three months. Keep picking them to encourage the plants to continue flowering.

A

B
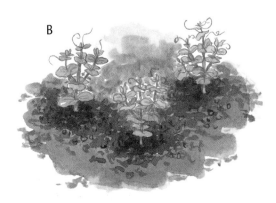

# Hiding an eyesore

EYESORES, such as oil tanks, old sheds, or unattractive chain-link fences, can soon be blended into the garden or completely disguised with vigorous climbing plants. There are a number of very different plants that can be used, from rambling roses to Japanese honeysuckles.

### HEAVY-DUTY COVER

The Russian vine (*Fallopia baldschuanica*) is one of the first climbers gardeners think of when faced with the problem of an ugly structure in their garden. When it has not only covered that unsightly shed, but completely filled it as well, they often regret their choice—so treat it with extreme caution. It is tough, fast growing, and trouble free, with hanging clusters of tiny white flowers in late summer. It will grow in any soil in sun or shade. If it wasn't so rampant, it would be the perfect plant for an unenthusiastic gardener. It is best to avoid it, though.

### RAMBLING ROSES

Some of the more vigorous rambling roses are perfect for covering up unsightly features. The following all have pretty, small white flowers and do a good job covering large structures in big gardens in the summer: 'Rambling Rector,' 'The Garland,' 'Mannington Cascade,' 'Seagull,' and *R. filipes* 'Kiftsgate.' It would be worth trying the following slightly less vigorous ramblers for their colored flowers: 'Treasure Trove' is creamy apricot, while 'Hiawatha' is a red single flower with a white eye, and 'Chevy Chase' has large clusters of small, deep crimson double flowers.

## COVERING WITH CLEMATIS

*Clematis montana* will cover a small building in three or four years, giving a spectacular and fragrant display of flowers in late spring and early summer. *C. m. grandiflora* has larger white flowers, *C. m. rubens* has pink flowers, *C. m.* 'Freda' has deep cherry-pink flowers and bronze foliage, and 'Tetrarose' has large pink flowers. Pruning is not normally necessary, but if they are getting too overgrown for comfort, prune immediately after flowering. 'Bill Mackenzie,' with its large flowers, is another good clematis for concealing unattractive structures, as is the late-flowering *C. orientalis*. It has pretty yellow flowers, followed by fluffy seed heads.

## LESS WELL-KNOWN PLANTS

There are many other good covering plants that are less well-known. They include:
• Moonseed (*Menispermum canadense*), a woody climber with blue-black berries in the fall. The handsome, circular leaves can be 8 in. across. It spreads by underground suckers and makes a good summer covering for unsightly sheds.
• Japanese honeysuckle (*Lonicera japonica* 'Halliana'), the related *L. j.* 'Hall's Prolific,' and *L. henryi* varieties are evergreen and very hardy.
• *Vitis coignetiae* is a vine grown for its enormous leaves, which turn a pink and apricot color in the fall.

*Vitis coignetiae* is among the most vigorous of vines and has large, heart-shaped leaves that turn shades of brilliant red, pink, and apricot in the fall. It makes a good screen.

• The golden hop (*Humulus lupulus* 'Aureus') is a fast, strong grower with attractive leaves. The leaves are quite rough, however, and if the plant is grown near a path, the stems can catch passersby unawares. This is an herbaceous climber that dies down in the winter months.
• Ivies, of course, are good at concealing things.
• 'Dutchman's Pipe' (*Aristolochia macrophylla*) has interesting curved green flowers, but these are often hidden by the leaves. The heart-shaped leaves get larger as they age. This plant must have moisture-retentive soil.

## COVER FOR CHAIN-LINK FENCES AND RAILINGS

For a perennial cover for chain-link fences and railings, the two Japanese honeysuckles, *Lonicera japonica* 'Halliana' and *L. j.* 'Hall's Prolific', are both good choices. The tendril climber Boston ivy (*Parthenocissus tricuspidata*) also makes a very dense screen and will cover very large areas. The honeysuckle has small but very scented flowers and the Boston ivy has good fall color.

The golden form of the climbing hop plant, *Humulus lupulus* 'Aureus,' grows well on a trellis. The twining stems need support and the new shoots should be woven through the trellis when they first appear each spring. This vigorous perennial has hanging clusters of "hops" in the fall and is a good choice for covering unsightly objects.

# Walls and fences

MANY CLIMBING PLANTS make an attractive cover for walls and fences of all types and are especially valuable if the boundary underneath is less than appealing. For solid walls in good condition, whether concrete, brick, or stone, self-clinging climbers such as ivy and Virginia creeper can save one the trouble of drilling to attach wires or a trellis. Some, however, can take a little time to cling properly and will benefit from support until they start to cling themselves.

If your wall or fence is relatively attractive, you can still enhance it with climbers; just choose less dense or vigorous plants. In these situations the climber should merely enhance its support, so pick the really pretty plants with a good show of flowers.

## SELF-CLINGING CLIMBERS FOR WALLS

Members of the hydrangea family are among the best self-clinging climbers, but they can be slow to get established. It is worth waiting, however, for they are magnificent plants and trouble free. *Hydrangea seemannii* has large, dark evergreen leaves and exciting heads of white flowers. It is not, however, as hardy as *Hydrangea anomala petiolaris* (the climbing hydrangea), which has similar flower heads made up of tiny, white fertile flowers surrounded by larger sterile flowers.

The flowers of schizophragma (*Schizophragma hydrangeoides* and *S. integrifolium*) have elegantly oval sepals at the end of each stem. *S. hydrangeoides* 'Moonlight' has leaves flushed with silver, while *S. h.* 'Roseum' has pink flowers.

*Pileostegia viburnoides* is evergreen and has small white flowers in panicles about 6 in. long. Another hydrangea relative, *Decumaria barbara*, will cling to a tree trunk but needs some support on a wall. The plant is deciduous or semievergreen and the flowers are scented but do not have showy leaves. *D. sinensis* is evergreen but less tolerant of cold.

## PLANTS FOR MOIST SHADE

*Ercilla volubilis* is an evergreen climber that likes moist shade and lime-free soil. It is good for a north wall, provided it is not too windy and the small, oval leaves will give a dense cover. The stems are long, gradually turning woody, and the whitish-pink flowers are produced in spikes in spring.

*Asteranthera ovata* is another evergreen that needs the same conditions. It has small crinkled leaves and large red trumpet flowers from summer onward and tends to spread sideways rather than grow upward.

The flower color of *Campsis grandiflora* varies between red and orange. Self-clinging, deciduous campsis are excellent for covering a warm wall.

### THE TRUMPET VINES

*Campsis*—the showy trumpet vines—are excellent for covering large walls and fences. They are deciduous and quite hardy, but need a sunny position to ripen the wood to produce their orange trumpets in summer. They can be cut back hard in winter and will produce long shoots in early summer, which soon attach themselves to a support by aerial roots.

- *Campsis* × *tagliabuana* 'Madame Galen' has wide-mouthed, orange-red, trumpet flowers.
- *C. radicans flava* has yellow trumpet flowers.
- *C. grandiflora* has deep orange or red trumpet flowers that are yellow inside.

## PLANTS FOR DRY SHADE

As mentioned on page 30, many ivies will do well in dry shade. Use a plain green ivy for a wall that fades into the background or a large-leaved, variegated ivy like *Hedera colchica* 'Sulphur Heart' to create a more dramatic backdrop.

*Euonymus fortunei* cultivars are best known as garden shrubs, with their glossy evergreen leaves, usually brightly colored in shades of green, lime, cream, and yellow. The less well-known *Euonymus fortunei radicans* will develop roots against a wall and scramble up it. These plants are useful as they will tolerate dry shade and are evergreen. Like ivy, they can be used where few other plants will grow (see page 58).

### DENSE GREEN COVER

If you want to turn your house completely green, Boston ivy (*Parthenocissus triscuspidata*) is the climber you need. The leaves of this vigorous plant are oval and have three lobes. The Boston ivy has splendid fall color and withstands a certain amount of drought. *P. t.* 'Lowii' has smaller, toothed leaves. *Parthenocissus henryana* has wonderfully subtle coloring, with velvety green leaves with silver veins and dark red undersides. In the fall it becomes deep scarlet. This plant is particularly good for shady walls.

## GARDEN KNOW-HOW

# Covering a fence

The evergreen honeysuckles *Lonicera japonica* 'Halliana' and the closely related 'Hall's Prolific' are fast-growing plants that will cover an unattractive fence quickly. For covering a chain-link fence in record time, these deliciously scented yellow- and white-flowered Japanese honeysuckles cannot be bettered. The small, tubular flowers appear in pairs in the leaf axils from midsummer to fall. If you are in a great hurry, buy one plant for every 24 in. of fence. Otherwise, space the plants out—one to every 3 ft. or even more. They are best planted in the spring.

1 Prepare the ground thoroughly, as described on page 10.

2 Plant the honeysuckles, packing them in well. The planting holes can be smaller than for many climbers; 8 x 8 in. is sufficient, unless you buy plants that are growing in large pots and have a larger rootball.

3 Thread the growing tips of the twining stems through the wire but leave one or two of them to grow along the ground, where they will soon root. You can help this process by placing small stones along the shoot so that it remains in contact with the ground.

4 When the shoots root themselves into the soil, which they do intermittently along their length, you can snip through the stems between each rooted section and each section will become a new plant.

5 Every four to five years the honeysuckle can be clipped back hard after flowering to form a dense screen.

### CARING FOR HONEYSUCKLE

Honeysuckles are very easy to grow and need little attention except for tidying up. Mulch lightly with leaf mulch or well-rotted compost every year in spring.

## ROSES FOR WALLS

Climbing roses are a classic choice for house walls, closely followed by clematis. They will need training on horizontal wires or trellis. When choosing a color, remember that strong pinks and reds do not always look their best against some types of bricks.

• R. 'Madame Alfred Carrière' is frequently recommended for shady walls; the color, white with a pink tinge, shows up well, and it is tolerant of most soils and conditions. This is a long–flowering rose, starting in summer and continuing through to the fall.

• R. 'Mermaid' is a single, yellow rose that will flower on a north wall.

The soft yellow flowers of the old tea rose, R. 'Climbing Lady Hillingdon,' show up to perfection on this old brick garden wall. 'Lady Hillingdon' needs a warm, protected wall to flower well and if tended to properly, will flower from summer until midwinter.

- Other roses that are often used on a shady wall successfully are R. 'Madame Grégoire Staechlin', a pretty bright pink; the once-flowering mauve R. 'Veilchenblau', and blush-pink 'New Dawn'.
- If you have a sunny wall, choose the rambling Banksian rose (R. banksiae var. banksiae), which is white. There is also a yellow version (R. b. 'Lutea'). It is vigorous, thornless, and has delicious clusters of frilly rosette flowers in May.
- R. 'Climbing Lady Hillingdon' has warm, yellow-apricot flowers, a wonderful spicy scent, and is also perfect for a sunny wall.

## SHRUB ROSES FOR WALLS OR PILLARS

Shrub roses can sometimes be trained against walls, even though they are not climbers. The Penzance briars like 'Meg Merrilees' and 'Lady Penzance' can be used to clothe a tripod. Bourbon roses such as 'Louise Odier', 'Reine Victoria', 'Madame Pierre Oger', and 'Madame Ernest Calvat' are shrub roses, but all will do well on pergolas, tripods, and trellises with the required support. Think twice about training Bourbon roses against walls, as they may succumb to mildew and black spot due to reduced airflow around their stems. 'Madame Pierre Oger' is a beautiful rose with double pink flowers, but it is particularly prone to these diseases.

"English" roses originate from crosses between the old-fashioned roses and modern varieties. They have been bred to combine the best features of each: The flowers are cup shaped or rosettes like the old varieties, with many small petals and a rich fragrance, but the color range is wider and they have more than one flush of flowers each year, characteristics they inherit from modern rose varieties. The taller English roses make excellent climbers for the small garden, as many grow to 6–8 ft. 'A Shropshire Lad' is a soft, peachy pink, 'Falstaff' is dark crimson, 'Graham Thomas' is a rich yellow, while 'Snow Goose' has white pom-pom flowers. 'Shropshire Lass' is a delicate flesh pink, while 'Constance Spry' has large pink flowers but blooms only once each year.

## CHOICE CLEMATISES

- Some of the large-flowered clematises, such as 'Nelly Moser', 'Lasurstern', 'Gipsy Queen', and 'Hagley Hybrid', may fade in hot sun and are best placed on walls that are shaded in the hottest part of the day.
- For sunny, sheltered walls, winter-flowering evergreen clematises are ideal. Try the large-leaved C. armandii with

## OTHER SUITABLE CLIMBERS

- Wisteria has long racemes of pea flowers in white or mauve, varying from 6–8 in. long in W. brachybotrys and its cultivars to 3–4 ft. in the Japanese wisterias (W. floribunda cvs).
- Actinidia kolomikta has slightly heart-shaped leaves, green but turning white with a pink flush in sunshine. The flowers are insignificant but the foliage is striking.
- Ampelopsis megalophylla has huge leaves and black berrries, and Ampelopsis glandulosa brevipedunculata has bright blue berries and shows up well against house walls.
- Take advantage of the warmth of south-facing walls to try semitender climbers like Solanum jasminoides 'Album,' Campsis tagliabuana 'Madame Galen,' the star jasmine (Trachelospermum jasminoides), or the passionflower (Passiflora caerulea).

white, sweetly scented flowers from early spring, C. a. 'Apple Blossom', which has pink buds that open to white, or C. a. 'Snowdrift', which has larger white flowers.
- In contrast, the leaves of Clematis cirrhosa are finely cut. C. c. balearica has cream bells speckled with brown. C. c. 'Wisley Cream' has creamy primrose bells and C. c. 'Freckles' has creamy-pink bells with red speckles.

## PLANTING CLIMBERS AGAINST WALLS

When planting against a wall, remember to prepare the ground at the foot thoroughly, as the soil is liable to dry out. Follow the instructions for preparing dry ground for planting on page 10.

The terrace or the border in front of the wall can be wide and well planted, using the wall simply as a background. Alternatively, the wall planted with climbing plants can dominate the scene and any border at the foot should be narrow and modest. An ordinary brick wall can be thickly planted with varieties of roses, for example, and have a simple line of lavender at the foot. An old stone wall might be better left almost bare as a restful background for a much wider, thickly planted border.

# Trellises

A TRELLIS CAN BE USED IN MANY DIFFERENT WAYS—to divide the garden up and create enclosed areas or to form arbors, covered structures, pillars, and obelisks. It is also frequently found as a simple support for climbing plants—attached to a wall, topping a wooden fence, or as a freestanding screen. It is a versatile feature that can be stained or painted in a variety of colors, but avoid overusing it in a garden or it will detract from the plants.

## ON A WALL

A trellis is often attached to a wall to support twining climbers, where it creates a geometric pattern across the surface. It is this pleasing geometry that makes a trellis a good supporter of a wide variety of climbing plants. Leaves and flowers, with their rounded forms and twining stems, contrast with it beautifully. It does need to be fixed carefully about 1 in. away from the wall to allow air circulation and room for the plants to be fixed on or twined through (for more information on this, see page 13).

## AS A DIVIDER

A trellis is a relatively cheap and easy way of dividing a garden, adding height and visual interest. It makes an attractive, lightweight barrier that allows light and air through—good for plants that are prone to mildew—and at close quarters you can see through it and glimpse areas of the garden beyond. It is perfect for the ornamental areas of the garden, but could also be used to support string beans and turn a vegetable garden into an enclosed and ornamental display.

*Clematis montana* makes a breathtaking sight in late spring, flowering luxuriantly and with unfailing regularity. This plant is getting slightly top-heavy for the trellis and will need cutting back immediately after flowering.

### TYPES OF TRELLISES

Trellis panels come in many different designs, some with a diagonal pattern, others square, some with a smaller mesh, and others larger. There are panels with curved tops or even panels with *trompe l'oeil* patterns such as a series of diminishing arches that create a false perspective. Avoid very cheap trellises, as you may find that just as the climbing plants become mature, the trellis will begin to fall apart. Always choose a trellis that has been pressure-treated with a wood preservative.

## SURFACE TREATMENTS

- If you leave the trellis in its natural color, it will go silvery in time and blends very pleasantly with any plant fixed to it.
- Painted white trellises are readily available, but white has its disadvantages in the garden. When new, it "jumps forward" and grabs your attention and as it gets older, it gets dirty and stained with lichen.
- Trellises can also be bought ready treated with a green wood preservative, which creates a subtle effect and goes well in most situations.
- There is a huge variety of brightly colored wood stains on the market and it is very tempting to play around with color and add dramatic effects yourself. You need to be careful, however, and choose colors that do not detract or clash with the plants. In cooler climates where the light levels are low, a dark blue–gray is good with rich red roses. A very dark green is a safe color, as are pale tones of ocher and terra-cotta.

Roses, red 'Galway Bay' and pink 'Clair Matin,' and a yellow honeysuckle make a not-quite-impenetrable screen behind a border.

## PLANTS FOR TRELLISES

- The honeysuckle *Lonicera similis* var. *delavayi*, which is not too vigorous, has a strong perfume and is reputed never to get aphids.
- Miniature climbing roses, such as *R.* 'Chewpixel' (Open Arms), and *R.* 'Chewizz' (Warm Welcome).
- "English" roses, such as 'Crown Princess Margareta,' which is a bright apricot–orange; 'Gertrude Jekyll,' rich pink; and 'Tess of the D'Urbervilles,' which is bright crimson.
- *Mauryandya barclayana*, with pinkish–purple snapdragon flowers.
- *Lophospermum scandens*, which has a range of pink, purple, white, and lavender flowers (often called *Asarina*).
- *Apios americana*, an unusual twining plant for a shady position. It is very hardy and flowers in late summer and early fall, with clusters of pea-shaped flowers variously described as maroon, chocolate, or blood–red.
- *Kadsura japonica*, an unusual evergreen twiner that has pale yellow flowers followed by round fruits resembling globes of scarlet berries. It is best in partial shade but needs a warm, sheltered spot and acid soil.

### COLOR SCHEMES

If the wall is painted and will need repainting in the future, then the trellis can be hinged, allowing it to be leaned forward and moved away from the wall without damaging the plants.

When painting or repainting a wall, think twice before using white masonry paint. As mentioned above, white tends to "jump out," shows every mark, and then tends to develop mold. Cream, pale sand, light gray, and pale pink all reflect the light well and are good backgrounds for many flowers. Rich colors like dark blue, green, and red are exciting with pale flowers growing against them. If the climbers you hope to grow have flowers that contrast with the wall color, it is better to paint any trellis in a toning shade, perhaps a little darker than the wall. The overall effect should not be overly decorative.

# Climbers as ground cover

CLIMBING PLANTS do not have to be grown up vertical surfaces. Some will grow happily along the ground and make dense and effective ground cover in difficult places. In fact, some plants even flower better when the stems are horizontal.

## PLANTS TO TRY

• Among the best are the ivies. Some of the larger-leaved ivies make excellent ground cover where nothing else will grow, such as in dry shade under trees. Try *Hedera canariensis* 'Ravensholst', *H. colchica* 'Dentata', *H. helix* var. *baltica*, and *H. h.* 'Green Ripple'.

• *Euonymus fortunei radicans* with its glossy, deep green oval leaves and the broad-leaved Irish ivy *H. Hibernica* will do well in dry, shady conditions.

• Several members of the rubus family, which also contains blackberries and raspberries, make a good ground cover when they have nothing to scramble up. *Rubus ichangensis* has panicles of white flowers, followed by edible fruits and semievergreen, glossy, tapered heart-shaped leaves. *R. irenaeus* has round leaves, up to 6 in. across, with a wavy edge, and small white flowers in summer followed by large red fruits. *R. lineatus* has a silvery sheen on the undersides of the leaves and distinctive parallel veins. *R. flagelliflorus* is graceful, with white-felted stems and shiny black fruits.

This shady corner in a town garden is stylish and almost maintenance free. The stone urn is surrounded by climbers grown as ground cover for a year-round effect. Tough, adaptable *Euonymus fortunei* 'Emerald 'n' Gold,' which will climb in the right circumstances, adds light and sparkle and contrasts with the large glossy leaves of the ivy.

- Everlasting pea (*Lathyrus latifolius*) can be allowed to sprawl over the ground. Unlike the annual sweet pea, the racemes of pinkish–purple flowers do not have to be picked regularly and they continue until the fall.
- *Anredera cordifolia* has highly fragrant racemes of white flowers in the fall and, although slightly tender, will regrow from the base in cooler climates. Alternatively, lift and store the tuberous roots like dahlias.
- Wood vamp (*Decumaria barbara*), a climbing hydrangea with white flower clusters and glossy oval leaves, is also good for ground cover.
- Clematis also flowers well when grown horizontally and can be grown with another ground cover plant.

## TRAINING ROSES

Training the shoots of climbing and rambling roses horizontally makes them flower right along their length instead of just at the tips. Some roses can be pegged right down to the ground to produce blooms at a low level. Long growths should be pegged to the ground in late summer. Any side shoots should be cut back to about 4 in. These will flower the following season, forming a pleasing mound covered with blooms. Try this with the following roses: 'Kathleen Harrop', 'Zéphirine Drouhin', and 'Martha', which are all thornless, or 'Blairii No. 2'.

## GARDEN KNOW-HOW

# Planting ivy as ground cover

Ivy, *Hedera sp.* and *cvs*, makes a good ground cover as it is tough, hardy, and evergreen. Requiring an almost neutral or alkaline soil, it roots as it goes and, after a slow start, will make a dense covering. There are many different types, and although variegations may not be as good in shade, if there is some sun, white, cream, or yellow variegated types can be used to create a rich tapestry.

1 The ground should be free from weeds, particularly perennial weeds like dandelion, docks, nettles, and ground elder. Dig these out carefully (A) or use an herbicide, following the manufacturer's instructions. If there is time, the ground can be covered with black plastic or old carpet for a season to smother the weeds (B).

2 Dig in some well-rotted manure, dried chicken manure, or compost (C).

3 Plant the ivy plants about 18 in. apart (D). The ivy can be trimmed over in subsequent years to keep it tidy.

**ALTERNATIVE METHOD**

Cover the ground with black sheet mulch. In early fall, take hardwood cuttings from an established ivy plant. They should be 6–8 in. long with the lower leaves removed. Make holes through the sheet and insert the cuttings so that one third of the length remains above the ground. These should be planted much closer together, approximately 10 in. apart. This method saves the need for weeding. In the first method, the ground will need to be kept clear of weeds until the plants have formed a dense cover.

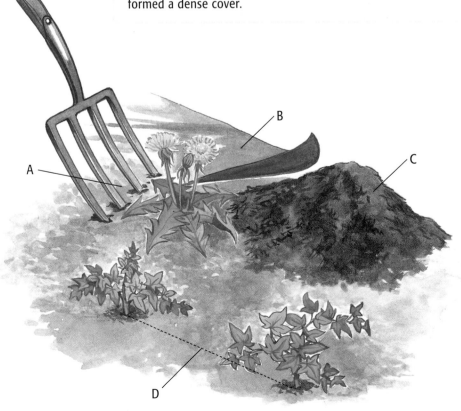

# CLASSIC COMBINATIONS

*I*n the wild, climbing plants grow over trees and shrubs. Growing climbing plants in this way allows you to get twice as many plants in the garden and extend the peak foliage season. In even the smallest garden there will be room for several clematises to scramble through the plants that are already there. In large gardens, trees that settle down to a dull middle age and an unexciting fall can be enlivened by growing a vigorous climbing rose or Virginia creeper into them. The Roman poet Horace noticed that the "beauteous marriageable vine" sometimes "to the lusty bridegroom elm does join." So many climbing plants have been introduced from continent to continent since then that there are wonderful combinations to try wherever you may be.

*Clematis* 'Perle d'Azur' scrambles over the evergreen *Bupleurum fruticosum* (shrubby hare's ear). The bupleurum has small, yellow flowers in clusters from midsummer to early fall and is an ideal companion for this not-too-vigorous blue clematis.

# Vigorous climbers for large trees

Vigorous climbers and large trees are a hungry combination, and to ensure success, be prepared to take your time with the planting and care of the climber, which is, after all, an interloper. Observe it at regular intervals for the first two years or so, until it is well established; it may need a boost now and then, perhaps with a foliar feed.

## PLANTING AGAINST A TREE

Plants that will grow up or into trees should be planted either right at the base of the tree, where there are very few feeding roots, or several yards beyond the edge of the tree's canopy, where the feeding roots diminish. To plant a climber to grow into an ash or sycamore, it is better to plant the climber beyond the canopy. Support the climber on canes or strings until it reaches the lower branches. Oak trees have deeper roots, as do cherry and apple trees, and the climber will do better if planted close to the trunk. To ensure success, dig a large hole, line the sides with plastic sheeting, and fill it with soil that has been enriched with organic matter.

## LARGE ROSES

The following large roses are suitable to be grown into a tree:
• Himalayan musk rose (*Rosa brunonii*) has single white flowers in clusters and stems that grow to 15–40 ft. long. *R. b.* 'La Mortola' is an even stronger grower.
• *R. filipes* is hardier and has clusters of a hundred or more small, creamy white flowers. The flower clusters on *R. f.* 'Kiftsgate' are even larger.
• White roses such as 'Bobbie James', 'Wedding Day', 'Rambling Rector', 'Toby Tristram', and *R. mulligani*.
• 'Paul's Himalayan Musk' is a soft pink.
• 'Easlea's Golden Rambler' is a rich yellow, as is 'Lawrence Johnson'.
• 'Desprez à Fleurs Jaunes' and 'Treasure Trove' are soft peachy–pink with yellow tones as well.
• 'Excelsa' is a light crimson.

## FOLIAGE CLIMBERS

The Virginia creeper (*Parthenocissus quinquefolia*) is one of the easiest and most successful climbers to grow into a tree. Very hardy, it attaches itself by adhesive pads on its tendrils. The leaves are in groups of five, like the fingers of a hand, and turn a glorious red in the fall. *Parthenocissus tricuspidata*, the

Boston ivy, is another self–clinging vigorous vine that colors spectacularly in the fall.

*Vitis coignetiae* is the most dramatic of the ornamental vines, reaching 60 ft. into a tree and then flowing down. The large leaves turn red in the fall. Other vines that can be encouraged to grow up through trees are *Vitis labrusca*, which will grow to 24–30 ft. and is very hardy, *V. davidii*, and *V. amurensis*.

## CLEMATISES FOR TREES

Clematises grow over trees in the wild and they really thrive when grown like this.
• *Clematis terniflora* is a very vigorous species and has white, scented bellflowers between late summer and midfall. This would make a good partner to a spring–flowering *C. montana* cultivar, like *C. m. grandiflora* over a large tree.

*Clematis montana* and a climbing rose were planted to mingle above this window, but the clematis much prefers the laburnum.

• *C. × vedrariensis* 'Rosea' is similar to *C. m.* 'Rubens', the pink-flowered montana, but the leaves bear some of the pale hairs associated with one of its parents, *C. chrysocoma*. The variety 'Hidcote' has small, deeper pink flowers. All of these will grow to 21–30 ft. in height.

• *Clematis flammula*, with white, star-shaped flowers from late summer to midfall, is another late bloomer that is good through trees.

• *C. armandii* has handsome elliptical leaves and white, scented flowers very early in the year.

• For warmer gardens, the winter-flowering *C. cirrhosa* will climb to 12 ft.

## OTHER VIGOROUS PLANTS

The American bittersweet, *Celastrus scandens*, is a deciduous, twining plant with pale yellow flowers that are followed by yellow berries in red-lined seed cases. *C. orbiculatus*, the Oriental bittersweet, is similar, but the flowers are pale green and it is more vigorous. To get the berries, you need to buy the hermaphrodite form and it will take about three years to settle in. The leaves of both turn yellow in the fall but *C. scandens* is more tolerant about position and drought. Both vines will need encouraging into the tree at first.

The long clusters of purple or white flowers of the wisterias look magnificent tumbling down from the canopy of a tall tree. Climbing hydrangeas and schizophragmas, with their large, white flower heads, are also splendid.

## Less common climbers for trees

• *Actinidia arguta*, from the same genus as the kiwi fruit, will grow to 60 ft. in a tree. It is very hardy and has small, white, fragrant flowers in summer followed (if two plants are grown) by edible oval fruits. These fruits, however, are not as tasty as the kiwi fruits that are sold commercially.

• *A. melanandra* has small, lance-shaped leaves with blue-white undersides on pink stalks and white flowers.

• *Akebia quinata*, the chocolate vine, is very fast growing and can be invasive. It has attractive foliage and vanilla-scented, chocolate-colored flowers.

• *Tripterygium regalii* grows to about 18 ft. It is an unusual climber with handsome oval leaves about 6 in. long. In late summer, panicles of small, white flowers are followed by greenish fruits with three wings.

The climbing hydrangea, *Hydrangea petiolaris*, will happily hoist itself into a tree or cling to a wall, but in both cases, it will need some encouragement for the first year or two.

### APPLE TREES

Gardeners lucky enough to have an orchard full of elderly apple trees can use these as supports for the less vigorous climbing and rambling roses, or taller old roses. Noisette roses and those derived from *R. wichurana* look beautiful grown in this way and come into bloom after the apple blossom has fallen and before the fruit itself makes a decorative contribution to the garden. Suitable roses include *R.* 'Climbing Cécile Brunner,' 'Alister Stella Gray,' 'Evangeline,' 'Dr. W. Van Fleet,' and 'Champney's Pink Cluster.'

# Climbers for scrambling over shrubs and hedges

COUNTRY HEDGEROWS USED TO HOST A TANGLE OF CLIMBERS–bryony, honeysuckle, Old Man's Beard, roses–and were beautiful to look at all year. Scrambling through shrubs and small trees is the natural way for many slender climbers to grow. In nature the plants put themselves where they want to be, often germinating in deep shade and finding their way to the sunny side of the shrub. They grow without any attention.

## PLANTING

Dig a planting hole, as described on page 10, at the outer edge of the shrub's canopy on the windward side. You want the wind to blow the climber toward the shrub and not away from it. It doesn't need to be more than 12 x 12 in. if the roots of the shrub are in the way. As with all other plants, make sure that the plant is thoroughly watered on a regular basis.

## PLANTS FOR DAPPLED SHADE

• *Codonopsis convolvulacea* is very good for scrambling through and over shrubs in the woodland garden. It has bell-shaped, light blue flowers and it likes dappled shade, as do *C. affinis*, with purple green bells, and *C. lanceolata*, which is larger and has green–purple bells with purple flecks inside. Codonopsis flowers in late summer and is ideal for adding interest to early summer flowering shrubs like deutzia, chaenomeles, and azaleas.

• The climbing monkshood *Aconitum hemsleyanum* can be grown easily from seeds, but it is better to buy a guaranteed dark blue plant from a nursery, as some seed-grown plants can often be an insipid mauve. It flowers nicely late from midsummer until the fall and the flowers go well with late-flowering shrubs such as escallonia, or with the red berries of a cotoneaster or the fruits of a berberis.

• The climbing fumitory *Adlumia fungosa* has fernlike leaves and drooping, pinkish-white flowers similar to those of a dicentra. Grow it from seed and plant out as soon as there are about six leaves. Grow it up a trained wall shrub such as pyracantha or chaenomeles.

• *Dicentra scandens* has bunches of pendant, yellow, slightly heart-shaped flowers tipped with pink or light purple and light, ferny foliage. It will twine through shrubs and can be cut back after the frosts. *D. macrocapnos* has similar flowers but is more vigorous.

• *Paederia scandens* is a hardy deciduous twiner with dark green leaves. Large panicles of small, creamy, tubular flowers with purple throats appear late in the year. *P. foetida* has lilac flowers and *P. tomentosa* has rose-purple flowers.

• The flame vine, *Tropaeolum speciosum*, flourishes in places with cool, damp summers and moist soil. It is often seen growing over yew hedges, which show off the vivid red flowers to perfection. The flowers are followed by deep blue fruits contrasting with purplish bracts. *T. azureum* is smaller, with blue flowers. *T. tuberosum* (of which the most widely available form is *T. t. lineamaculatum* 'Ken Aslet') has blue-green leaves and long-spurred, orange-red flowers. *T. tricolorum*, which grows to about 4 ft., is for warmer climates only and has striking orange or yellow flowers from red-orange, black-tipped calyces (the outer protective part of the flower consisting of fused sepals that form a tube).

## PLANTS FOR SUN

• *Billardiera longiflora* has long, lime-yellow flowers in later summer, followed by vivid violet-blue berries. It needs wall protection and full sun or can be grown in a container and taken inside in the winter.

• *Dichelostemma volubile* is a half-hardy perennial that grows from a swollen root. The allium-like leaves can be 24 in. long and the flowering stem, over 3 ft. The stem twines through its host shrub so that the pink flowers are in the sun. A shrub border against a south wall would suit it but it still needs protection from the frost.

• Moonseed, *Menispermum canadense*, has large round leaves on long stalks. The flowers are an inconspicuous greenish–white and are followed by small, black fruits.

• The Chilean glory flower, *Eccremocarpus scaber*, with orange, red, or yellow flowers, is an annual or short–lived perennial climber that will scramble over small shrubs.

Most of these climbers die back at the end of the year and can be tidied up then. *Eccremocarpus* dies back to a small tuber and can be either dug up like a dahlia or mulched. *Billardiera* can be planted out in a pot that has been sunk into the ground. This can then be brought into a frost–free place during the winter.

The vivid red flowers and pretty, five-lobed leaves of *Tropaeolum speciosum*, the flame creeper from Chile, show up beautifully against dark yew, *Taxus baccata*.

## A LIVING SUPPORT

Using one climber to support another is a good way of extending the season of interest throughout the year. Vines, especially *Vitis* species, are useful for this. They are fast growing and soon produce a woody framework capable of supporting some of the less-vigorous flowering climbers. Ornamental vines are often at their best in late summer and the fall, when they are fruiting and the leaves color, so they make good companions for early-flowering climbers like *Clematis alpina* and *C. macropetala*. Suitable species are *Vitis davidii*, *V. riparia*, *V. thunbergii*, and *V. labrusca*. *V. parvifolia* is particularly charming, with copper-colored new foliage and small but profuse, glossy green-bronze leaves in summer. Its rich fall color is accompanied by tiny, blue-tinged black fruits. Do not try to grow anything over fruiting grapevines, as these need all the air and sunshine they can get.

All pruning should be carried out in winter before the sap rises. Train the vine to form a permanent framework and cut back to one or two buds to form a spur system, which becomes more attractive with age. Excessive growth should be stopped at five to six leaves in midsummer, and this often means that there are leaves of different ages, which is a pleasant contrast. A vine's support systems need to be very sturdy, and tall enough as they grow quickly in the season (see pages 70–73 for detailed information on training and caring for vines).

# Clematis couples

CLEMATISES ARE VERY "LIGHT" CLIMBERS and can be trained with and over many other plants, such as honeysuckle, roses, vines, or climbing hydrangea, without damaging them. They can be grown in pairs and even the smallest garden has room for one or two. However, they need careful planting to look their best, and pruning can be complicated (see pages 20–21).

## COMBINING CLEMATISES

If you plan to plant your clematises in pairs, it will be less trouble if you choose two plants that both need the same pruning regime. You can mix two late, large-flowering hybrids like purple-red 'Ernest Markham' and white 'Huldine', which both need lots of sun to flower well, or the blue 'Perle d'Azur' with shell-pink 'Hagley Hybrid', both of which will take more shade.

For a late-flowering combination in a sunny position, 'Madame Baron Veillard' is a bright lilac-pink and would combine well with a viticella cultivar like 'Venosa Violacea'. Two early-flowering clematises that would look good together are *C. alpina* 'Helsingborg', which is deep purple, and *C. a.* 'Ruby', which is a soft red. Neither of these need pruning.

When planting, make the planting hole (see page 10) twice as deep, rather than twice as wide, and add a thick layer of well-rotted organic matter at the base, since you will be feeding two plants. Make sure that the surface of the rootballs are at least 3 in., and preferably closer to 6 in., below soil level.

## CLEMATIS WITH OTHER CLIMBERS

Clematis can be grown with other climbers, too.
• The purple leaves of *Vitis vinifera* 'Purpurea' look sumptuous with *Clematis* 'Etoile Violette' or 'Ernest Markham'.
• Silver- or white-variegated ivies form a good background for shade-tolerant, blue *C.* 'William Kennett' and bright pink *C.* 'Scartho Gem', which has a deeper bar.
• Another good combination for shade is the climbing hydrangea (*Hydrangea anomala petiolaris*) with rosy-lilac *C.* 'Comtesse de Bouchaud'.
• *C.* 'Gravetye Beauty' has ruby-red flowers until midfall, which show up well against silver-leaved shrubs.
• Other good contrasts are yellow *C.* 'Bill Mackenzie' with the late-flowering perennial pea *Lathyrus latifolius* or the golden hop, *Humulus lupulus* 'Aureus'.

• *C. tangutica* with the climbing monkshood, *Aconitum hemsleyanum*, which is blue.
• Rose 'Golden Showers' with violet-purple *C.* 'Etoile Violette'.
• Rose-crimson *C.* 'Kermesina' or the large, lavender-blue flowers of *C.* 'Lasurstern' are very pretty against yellow-variegated ivies such as *Hedera helix* 'Oro di Bogliasco'.
• The self-clinging Virginia creeper (*Parthenocissus quinquefolia*) will support any of the clematises and provide a handsome backdrop of foliage.

## CLEMATIS WITH SHRUBS

Woody wall shrubs like the Japanese quince (*Chaenomeles*) or wall-trained pyracanthas are perfect hosts for clematis. Choose clematises that flower at different times to their host shrubs to extend the season of interest. The Japanese quince blooms early on old wood and can be kept trimmed back, allowing the clematis to display its flowers well. Use the quince as a host for summer-flowering, large-flowered clematis. You could even increase the succession of flowers against the wall by adding a late-flowering *C. viticella* cultivar.

## CONTRASTING SHAPES

Contrasting colors are very eye-catching, but a contrast of shapes in similar colors also works very well. There are many possibilities:
• *Clematis montana* and *Rosa* 'Sombreuil'.
• *Rosa* 'Climbing Iceberg' with the pretty, small-flowered *C.* × *triternata* 'Rubromarginata', which has rosy-red edges to the petals.
• Blue wisteria with *C.* 'Perle d'Azur'.
• White *Wisteria sinensis* and *Clematis montana*. They are both very hardy and vigorous.

These pictures show the different effects that can be created when the same clematis is paired with different plants. The picture above shows *Clematis* 'Perle d'Azur' paired with *Rosa* 'Morning Jewel'; this coupling is very harmonious. The image on the right shows the vibrant blue of the clematis contrasting with golden hop *Humulus lupulus* and *Lonicera* 'Graham Thomas.'

## COMPARING COLORS

Most container-grown clematises will be in bloom when you see them in the garden center or nursery. It is easy to check color combinations by doing what Vita Sackville West used to do at Sissinghurst. Carry the plant around and put it beside its prospective companion to see how it looks. Even if one climber is supposed to come into bloom just as another has gone over, this does not always go according to plan, so it is helpful if the colors pleasantly enhance each other.

# EDIBLES

*C*limbing plants that produce edible fruits or vegetables fit well into the kitchen garden, turning a utilitarian vegetable plot into an ornamental display. When properly supported, both annual and perennial climbers can be used to create enclosures, provide shelter from wind, and create light shade, and are decorative and fruitful.

Annual fruits and vegetables, such as squashes and string beans, add instant height to flower beds and form screens very quickly. They can have a different position in the garden every year. Others, like vines and brambles, are more permanent features in the productive garden.

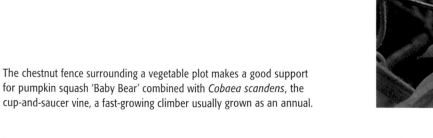
The chestnut fence surrounding a vegetable plot makes a good support for pumpkin squash 'Baby Bear' combined with *Cobaea scandens*, the cup-and-saucer vine, a fast-growing climber usually grown as an annual.

# Grapevines

THERE ARE MANY SPECIES OF VINES that are purely ornamental, and these are referred to in other chapters. In this chapter, the emphasis is on the fruiting vine, *Vitis vinifera*, and its cultivars and hybrids. Grapevines are adaptable plants and tougher than many people realize. You can grow them for their fruit as you see them in commercial vineyards, sometimes with only a short leg and one long stem on each side. In a sunny, sheltered vegetable garden, such vines make attractive edgings to the beds.

Conversely, you can grow a grapevine as an ornamental, enjoying its attractive leaves. Vines in Mediterranean countries are often used as shade providers, trained over pergolas and arbors. They still produce fruit, the long bunches of grapes hanging down invitingly from the roof, but not so intensively. In cooler climates many varieties need to be grown against a warm, sunny wall or under glass to produce edible fruit, but not all. Many vines are quite hardy, especially those derived from the American *V. labrusca*.

## PLANTING

Grapes must have a sheltered, sunny site. Choose the site carefully, prepare the ground, and ensure good drainage by adding gravel or sand to the enriched soil (see pages 10–11). On very acid soil, add lime; on a poor soil, add plenty of well-rotted garden compost.

Year-old vines should be planted in the winter, 4–5 ft. apart. If you are planting a single vine against a wall, position it 9 in. from the wall. Each plant will need a vertical cane or post as a support. Spread the roots out well, then fill the hole with soil and firm in well. Prune the vine down to two good buds from ground level. In early spring, apply a general fertilizer and then mulch each plant with well-rotted compost.

## SUPPORTING THE VINES

Grapes need supporting on wires, whether they are grown in the open or against a wall, and the wires need to be put in place before the vines are planted. In the open, erect 6-ft. wooden posts about 8 ft. apart, sinking them 24 in. into the ground. Metal post supports are also ideal for this purpose as they can be hammered into the ground and the posts bolted into them. Stretch three horizontal wires at 1-ft. intervals between the posts, with the lowest 18 in. above the ground. Fix the wires securely in place with staples. Plant the vines at least 8 ft. apart.

The grapevine growing over this barn is allowed to do its own thing and is more decorative than fruitful.

### GRAPES FOR WALLS

- *V.* 'Himrod' is a seedless variety of golden grape.
- *V.* 'Triomphe d'Alsace' is a black grape suitable for dessert or wine.
- *V.* 'Léon Millot' has black grapes and is very reliable. Its vigor makes it a good decorative vine to grow against a wall.
- *V. v.* 'Chasselas' has white, well-flavored fruit and must be grown on a warm wall.
- The strawberry grape, *V.* 'Fragola,' has red fruits that smell of strawberries.

# Training a grapevine

These instructions show how to train a grapevine on wires to produce the maximum amount of fruit. If you do not want to embark on such a complicated regime and are just growing one grapevine against a wall or over a pergola, remember that grapevines produce their fruit on shoots growing from one-year-old stems. If the vine is not pruned and trained at all, it will soon become a tangle. Aim to produce a permanent woody framework that encourages the yearly production of new wood.

1 In the spring, plant the vine you have bought from a garden center or nursery. Allow one shoot to develop during the summer and train it vertically up the post or cane. Pinch other shoots back to one leaf.

2 In late fall, cut the vine down again to within 18 in. of the ground, leaving just three buds (A).

3 The following spring, three shoots will grow and these should be trained vertically. If any side shoots appear, pinch them back to one leaf.

4 In the fall of that year, tie down one of the shoots to the left and another to the right, along the wires. Cut them back to about 30 in. long. Cut the central stem back to three buds (B).

5 In the summer of the subsequent year, those three buds will grow into three new stems and these should be trained vertically. The horizontal stems will develop laterals that will grow vertically and bear fruit (C). In the first fruiting year, do not allow the vine to carry more than two or three bunches of grapes; during the next season, they can be allowed to bear four or five, and after that they can bear a full crop.

6 In the fall, these fruit-bearing horizontals must be pruned back and the vertical shoots from the center will provide the replacements, which should be pruned and tied in as before (D).

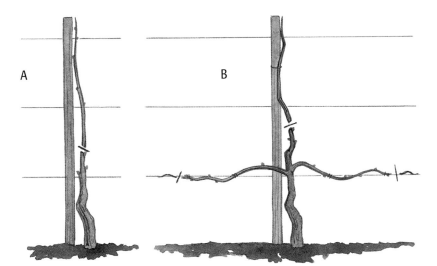

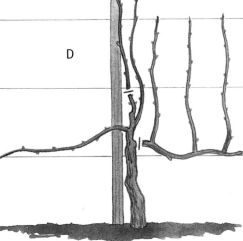

# A standard grapevine

A standard grapevine does not take up too much room and can be grown either in the ground or in a pot that can be moved in and out of a greenhouse. Grapevines need a cold period during the winter, but the fruit needs a long, warm ripening period and a container-grown vine makes this possible in many areas.

1 Take a year-old vine and plant it in a 7-in. pot with some crocks at the base, filled with John Innes No. 3 compost. Alternatively, plant it in a prepared planting hole in the ground (see page 10). Choose the hottest site you can find, but not one that is too sheltered, as grapes need air circulation. In late fall, cut the main stem back to a bud about 6 in. from the compost.

2 The following spring and summer, train the vine up a cane and pinch the side shoots back to one leaf (A).

3 Next winter, cut the stem back to a bud 3–5 ft. above the compost, depending on the height you want your standard vine to be. Repot the plant into a 15-in. pot and remove all the side shoots (B).

4 In the following summer, let four or five shoots develop from the top, but stop them when they have made five or six leaves. Continue to keep the stem clear, and remove any flowers if necessary.

5 That winter, prune each of the four or five shoots back to one bud (C). Repot the vine again, this time into an 18-in. pot. Keep the vine securely staked.

6 In the subsequent season, let the vine produce two bunches of grapes and pinch out the branches at two leaves beyond the fruit. The other laterals should be pinched back to five leaves and any sublateral shoots back to one leaf (D).

A

B

C

D

## MAKING YOUR OWN PLANTS

If you already have a vine, prunings root very easily. These are cheap and fun to use for different growing methods. Take a 10- to 12-in. hardwood pruning, trimmed above and below a bud, and insert it into the ground to two thirds of its length in a sheltered spot in sandy soil in midfall.

In this garden a vine has been used as an ornamental, trained attractively over an arch.

## CARING FOR YOUR STANDARD VINE

The compost should never be allowed to dry out. Top dress the soil each winter by removing the top 1 in. of soil in the container and replacing it with fresh compost. In the open ground, mulch around the base of the grapevine with compost or well-rotted manure. In the first year, apply a liquid feed every week until late summer. In subsequent years, do this until the fruit has set. You can help the flowers to fertilize themselves by shaking the vine gently when it is in bloom. Bunches of fruit may need thinning out.

### GRAPES FOR PERGOLAS, ARBORS, ARCHES, POSTS, AND WIRES

- *V.* 'Brant' has small bunches of black grapes and is particularly attractive when the leaves turn red in the fall.
- *V. labrusca* 'Concord' is a popular American grape.
- *V.* 'Boskoop Glory' is black, sweet, and good for dessert.
- *V.* 'Cascade' (syn. *V.* 'Seibel 13053') is an early black grape, prolific and reliable.
- *V. vinifera* 'Incana' has leaves and stems covered in a fine gray-white down.
- *V. v.* 'Madeleine Angevine 7672' is a dessert grape that is also used for wine.
- *V. v.* 'Siegerrebe' has golden berries and a muscat flavor.
- *V. v.* 'Madeleine Sylvaner 28/51' is a white grape for dessert and wine.
- *V. v.* 'Perlette' needs some thinning of its white, seedless grapes as the bunches can get overfull of fruits.

# Cane fruits

CLIMBING CANE FRUITS ARE very useful garden plants. Like ornamental climbers, the long stems they produce can be used on supports to give height in a garden, to grow through something else, or to clothe a wall. Blackberries, loganberries, boysenberries, tayberries, and other blackberry crosses are all useful and provide delicious fruit. There are other, more unusual cane fruits like the Japanese wineberry (*Rubus phoenicolasius*), which is particularly ornamental. The edible fruits are small, garnet-red, and usually free from pests. The fruits of *Rubus flagelliflorus*, *R. setchuenensis*, *R. spectabilis*, and *R. ichangensis* are edible, although these canes are usually grown for their ornamental qualities.

## PRUNING AND TRAINING CANE FRUITS

Most cane fruits can be trained against a trellis, a freestanding post, or wire fencing (see "A Blackberry Screen," opposite), or they can be left to naturally arch over.

1. Buy certified virus-free plants. Plant them shallowly in a sunny, but not exposed, position. Blackberries fruit on one-year-old wood, so fruiting canes need to be kept separate from new canes. Train older canes to one side and new ones to the other.

2. At the end of winter, remove the old canes by cutting them down to the ground.

3. Pick up the new canes and tie them onto the wires, trellis, or other support, leaving an equal distance between them.

4. The canes can be fanned out simply, or woven in any number of ways.

## CARING FOR CANE FRUITS

Plant the fruits 6–8 ft. apart, according to variety, in the fall. The following spring, scatter a compound fertilizer in the amount suggested on the packet, in a circle 18 in. in diameter around each plant, and rake it in lightly. Repeat this at the end of May and the end of June. In following years, mulch each spring with well-rotted manure.

Raspberry beetles, gray mold, and birds may be problems. To prevent the problem of raspberry beetles, spray a derris-based insecticide at dusk when the blackberry flowers begin to open. For gray mold, keep plants clear of dead and dying material and provide good air circulation. If birds are especially troublesome, netting the plants is the answer.

### CHOOSING PLANTS FOR A SCREEN

Plants with long, flexible canes are necessary and as there is much handling of the stems involved, thornless cultivars make the undertaking easier.

• *Rubus fruticosus laciniatus* 'Oregon Thornless' is slightly smaller than some other cultivars. Although it is a useful size for a medium garden, the stems are quite stout and need careful handling to weave them well.

• Other thornless varieties are: *R. fruticosus* 'Thornfree,' *R. f.* 'Merton Thornless,' and *R. f.* 'Waldo.'

• The hybrid *Rubus* 'Boysenberry, Thornless' is good on light soils and is very drought resistant and much less vigorous than blackberries.

• The fruits of loganberries can be up to 2 in. long and *Rubus* (Loganberry Group) 'LY 654' is thornless.

• *Rubus phoenicolasius* (the Japanese wineberry) is very attractive and the red bristles on the stems are not too sharp to handle, although gloves are recommended.

The Japanese wineberry, *Rubus phoenicolasius*, has attractive fruits, stems covered with red hairs, and pale green leaves felted white on the underside.

## A Blackberry Screen

Blackberry canes can be woven to make an attractive screen, from which it is much easier to pick the fruit than the usual tangled mass of stems. Loganberries, boysenberries, and Japanese wineberries can also be trained in the same way.

1 Sink two 9-ft. posts firmly into the ground, 8 ft. apart, and stretch wires horizontally between them. Starting at about 3 ft. from the ground, you will need a wire every 12 in.

2 Plant the canes between the two posts in winter, spacing them at 8-ft. intervals. Cut the plants back to a bud, 10 in. above the ground (A).

3 In early spring, fork some general fertilizer, such as pelleted chicken manure or blood, fish, and bone, into the soil around the plants.

4 A month later, mulch the plant with well-rotted garden compost, but do not let the compost touch the canes.

5 New canes will appear in summer and should be woven in and out of the wires (B).

6 In the following year, fruit will be carried on laterals of the previous year's canes. The new canes should be trained up through the center of the bush and tied in to the top wire (C).

7 In the fall, after fruiting, all the fruited canes should be cut back to the base and the new canes rewoven to take their place.

A

B
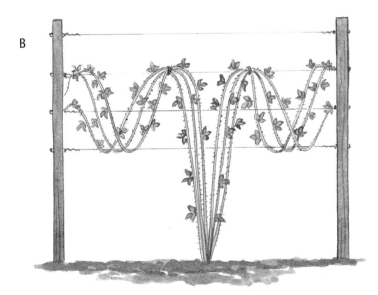

C

# Cucurbits

THE CUCURBIT FAMILY CONTAINS many of the well-known climbing fruiting plants, including melons, cucumbers, pumpkins, and squashes. These are all attractive plants with large, handsome leaves and impressive, delicious fruits. They climb by means of tendrils, or will happily scramble over the ground and any obstacles they come across.

Also in this family are about twenty-five species of tropical and subtropical plants that are interesting and attractive to grow, as well as being useful, although inedible. In a warm climate or under glass, grow your own loofah (*Luffa cylindrica*) or calabash (*Lagenaria vulgaris*).

## GROWING CUCURBITS

Pumpkins and squashes are generally allowed to ramble over the ground because the fruits become so heavy. Some ornamental gourds and squashes, however, can be grown up wigwams or over pergolas and arches. They look splendid in a vegetable garden grown this way. Melons and cucumbers are generally grown as climbing plants. Against a wall, the fruits ripen better and they can be kept away from damp soil and pests more easily.

All these plants are grown as annuals in more or less the same way and they need good, rich, moisture-retaining soil. Sow the seeds in pots in early spring. The temperature needs to be about 68°F in order for them to germinate properly, so a heated propagator may be necessary. Plants can be moved outside in the middle of spring or grown in a greenhouse border.

## Cucumbers

Cucumber seeds need to be sown on their sides. Train the stems up canes and pinch out the growing point when the plant reaches the roof of the greenhouse. Pinch out the side shoots at two leaves beyond a female flower (the one that has a small cucumber behind it). The plants need a moist atmosphere and regular feeding with a tomato fertilizer. Outdoor cucumbers can be left to scramble on the ground– protect the plants with straw and plastic to keep the fruits clean–or grown up supports.

## Melons

Melons are grown indoors in cool climates, like indoor cucumbers, but need a warmer temperature. Watering should be restricted to when the fruits are ripening to ensure a good flavor. The flowers will need hand-pollinating: Use a small, clean paintbrush to transfer the pollen from a male to a female flower (which has a distinct swelling immediately behind the petals), then remove the male flower immediately afterward. The fruits will need supporting in loose netting bags as they get heavier.

## Zucchini and squash

Zucchini, squash, gourd, and pumpkin seeds need to be kept at a temperature of 59°F to germinate well. If the seeds are sown outdoors, sow two or three in each position after all danger of frost has passed and cover the seeds with a cloche or a jelly jar. When they germinate, thin out to one plant at each position, discarding the weaker seedlings, and allow about 3 ft. between plants. Water and feed regularly. Zucchini should be picked regularly to encourage further fruiting.

## GROWING GOURDS OVER AN ARCH

Growing gourds over an arch shows off the brightly colored fruits, which hang down prettily as bunches of grapes and wisteria flowers do. Small, ornamental gourds are best because they are not too heavy; come in a variety of patterns, colors, and shapes; and can be left on the plant for a long time. If space is tight it is possible to grow zucchini in this way, but because they are grown for eating, the display is continually diminished.

The ideal arches for growing gourds over are the painted metal ones that can be bought in garden centers. They are not too expensive and are easy to erect as they come with long metal "legs" that are sunk into the ground. Choose ones with crosspieces up the side, which are used for the gourd's tendrils to twine around.

The Turk's cap gourd is particularly decorative grown over an arch. As the fruits get larger, they may need supporting.

Gourds grown over a fence are a decorative way of separating the vegetable plot from the rest of the garden.

# Other produce

THERE ARE OTHER FRUITS PRODUCED on climbing plants, like kiwi and passion fruit, that will grow in temperate climates. The plants are vigorous and relatively hardy but need some care to fruit well. At the other extreme are the humble peas and beans, which make good, quick screens.

## KIWI FRUIT

The kiwi fruit or Chinese gooseberry (*Actinidia deliciosa*) is very vigorous and needs a considerable amount of space. In cool regions it needs to be grown on a warm wall, but where the weather is warmer it looks magnificent on a well–built pergola. Most actinidia need male and female plants to produce fruit. The late–flowering variety 'Hayward' can be paired with 'Tomari', which flowers at the same time. However, new cultivars have been bred that are self-fertilizing, like 'Jenny' and the much hardier *A. arguta* 'Issai', which has fragrant flowers and bunches of small fruits.

## Training kiwis

After planting, cut the kiwi fruit back to about 12 in. above the ground. Fruiting actinidias are trained like grapevines and need the same system of strong horizontal wires and vertical canes or posts (see pages 70–71).

Tie the stem to the cane and allow side shoots to grow along the horizontal wires. Remove all other shoots. When the horizontal shoots are 3 ft. long, stop them. This will encourage the production of lateral shoots. Stop the laterals at five leaves to encourage the growth of fruit–bearing spurs.

In the third summer, the plant should begin fruiting. All fruiting branches should be pinched back to seven leaves after the last fruit. Pinching back laterals without any fruit to five leaves will encourage them to produce fruiting spurs. All extra laterals and sublaterals should be removed.

### KIWIS ON PERGOLAS

In warm regions, kiwi fruits can be attractively trained over a pergola, as they will not need the shelter of a warm wall. The kiwi fruit should be allowed to develop a single main stem up to the top of the pergola, with two leaders trained along the top in opposite directions. The fruiting branches are trained at right angles to the leaders, across the top. The laterals that bear the fruit hang down from the roof.

## PASSION FRUIT

The passion fruit (*Passiflora edulis*) is the best-known species of the edible passionflowers. It is not hardy in all areas; it fruits reliably when grown under glass or with a minimum temperature of 50°F and with a temperature of at least 61°F during the flowering period.

### POLLINATION

Under glass and in temperate zones, passionflowers will need hand-pollinating. Using a clean paintbrush, transfer the pollen from the anthers of one flower to the stigma of another. *P. incarnata*, *P. quadrangularis*, and *P. alata* do not readily self-pollinate, so it is necessary to grow two or more plants. The yellow-fruited *P. edulis flavicarpa* can only be cross-pollinated by its purple sibling, *P. edulis*.

## How to grow passion fruit

Passion fruit can be grown from seeds, cuttings, or from grafted plants. The plants need to be supported on a trellis attached to sturdy uprights sunk into the ground. Prepare the soil by adding well-rotted manure or other organic matter and a high-nitrogen fertilizer. Plant the vines about 10–12 ft. apart. Allow fruiting branches to cascade toward the ground. Keep the plants well watered and cut back hard after the second year. Add mulch or organic manure every fall.

Under glass, plants can be grown in containers at least 14 in. across, or in a prepared greenhouse or conservatory bed in well-drained, fertile compost with plenty of organic matter. They will need to be supported on a trellis or by wires. Train two main stems along wires and pinch out the growing tips when the stems are 24–36 in. long. The fruiting laterals will droop toward the ground. Cut back the fruiting stems after they have fruited. Mulch and water as above. Passion fruits are susceptible to a virus that causes woodiness in the fruit, so plants need to be replaced on a regular basis.

## PEAS AND BEANS

Where space is limited, climbing beans and peas have many advantages, as they take up little room. They are also attractive enough to grow in ornamental areas, with their large leaves, red, white, or lilac flowers, and handsome, long pods. They need supporting, first with twiggy sticks, then on canes or pea and bean netting, but they crop well and will provide shelter for more tender crops.

## Growing beans

Both climbing French beans and string beans are available and can be sown outdoors in their growing positions when any danger of frost has passed and the soil has warmed up. Earlier in the year, they can be sown under cloches, in pots on a windowsill, or in a greenhouse.

Sow French beans about 2 in. deep and 8 in. apart. Scarlet runner beans are very prolific but need better soil than French beans. Dig the soil deeply and add plenty of

String beans, *Phaseolus coccineus*, are both decorative and effective grown over arches of bent branches linked with one crosspiece to give stability.

manure in the fall before sowing. Start as for French beans but sow 2–3 in. deep, 6 in. apart. When the seedlings are growing, remove every other seedling, leaving 12 in. between each plant.

The whole pods can be eaten when they are young or alternatively, leave them on the plants so the beans ripen and can be used like navy beans. Try doing some of each, an economical method when the beans are all becoming ready at the same time.

### DECORATIVE BEANS

There are several different colors available that make a very decorative addition to the garden. These plants may not produce as many beans as plain green varieties.
- For **deep purple** beans, try 'Cosse Violette.'
- For **yellow** beans, grow 'Corona d'Oro' or 'Meraviglia di Venesia.'
- For **green with red splashes**, try 'Barlotta Lingua di Fuoco.'
- For **red and white** flowers, you need to grow 'Painted Lady.'
- For **white** flowers, try 'Mergoles.'

### SUPPORTING BEANS

To make a dense screen of beans, sow two rows, 8 in. apart for French beans or 12 in. apart for string beans, with the plants staggered. Alternatively, grow the beans up a wigwam of canes. This method is particularly suitable if you are growing the beans in a container.

## Growing peas

The taller varieties of peas also make useful screens and are grown in a similar way to beans. Dig plenty of manure or compost into the soil. Sow the seeds 1 in. deep, 2–3 in. apart. Main crop peas, like 'Alderman' or 'Show Perfection,' grow to about 5 ft. 'Pilot,' another tall variety, is extremely hardy. The 'Carouby de Maussane' variety is a tall growing snow pea that will reach 5 ft., as will 'Sugar Snap,' which can also be eaten pod and all. For something really wdifferent, try 'Ezetha's Krombek Blauwschok,' which has beautiful violet flowers and pods and grows to 6 ft.

# PLANTS FOR WARM PLACES

*This chapter looks at some of the tempting climbers that will grow outdoors in warm climates, but need protection and additional heat in cooler regions in the form of a greenhouse.*

*For some climbing plants, humidity as well as high temperatures are needed. Many tropical climbers need shade, too: They are native to tropical rain forests and these conditions are difficult to reproduce artificially without a large expenditure of money and effort. Many tropical climbers are also extremely vigorous. In their native habitat they grow to the tops of huge trees, festooning the canopies and flowering out of sight. Choosing the right plants for your conditions is as important in warm climates or a greenhouse as it is in cooler ones.*

Brilliant bougainvillea looks at its best against Mediterranean-blue skies and white-painted houses, but it can be grown in a greenhouse.

# Choosing the right plants

CHOOSING THE RIGHT PLANT is as important in a greenhouse or warm climate as it is elsewhere. Wonderful plants such as the Jade vine, *Strongylodon macrobotrys*, with long racemes of pea flowers with keels in an exquisite shade of pale green unfortunately have to be resisted if you do not own a few acres of rain forest or have a large, dedicated greenhouse where such a climate can be replicated. Something less showy that grows well will be much more satisfying.

## CLIMATE ZONES

All of the plants listed in the Plant Directory (see pages 88–93) are given climate zones, which indicates the temperature range they will thrive in.

| CLIMATE ZONE | Average Minimum Temperature |
|---|---|
| ZONE 1 | -50°F |
| ZONE 2 | -50° to -40°F |
| ZONE 3 | -40° to -30°F |
| ZONE 4 | -30° to -20°F |
| ZONE 5 | -20° to -10°F |
| ZONE 6 | -10° to 0°F |
| ZONE 7 | 0° to 10°F |
| ZONE 8 | 10° to 20°F |
| ZONE 9 | 20° to 30°F |
| ZONE 10 | 30° to 40°F |
| ZONE 11 | over 40°F |

## WARM SPOTS OUTSIDE

There are many wonderful, exotic climbing plants that will cope with a slight chill now and then. These are climbers that originate from the Mediterranean, from parts of Australia, California, and South America. In northern temperate regions, plants described as hardy in zone 9 may well survive in sheltered town gardens or if grown against south-facing walls. *Araujia sericofera, Clematis armandii, C. cirrhosa* var. *balearica, C. texensis, Eccremocarpus scaber, Passiflora antioquiensis, Solanum jasminoides* "Album," *Sollya heterophylla*, and *trachelospermums* are all on the borders of hardiness.

## WINTER PROTECTION

In a really cold spell, the roots of tender plants can be protected with a thick mulch; a mixture of straw, bracken, dead leaves, and wood shavings will suffice.

Evergreen plants are more likely to be killed by frost than deciduous climbers. The well-ripened framework of a

Evergreen *Clematis armandii* flowers in early spring. It is one of the more tender clematises and needs the protection of a warm wall to flower so luxuriantly.

woody climber like *Campsis radicans* can withstand a surprising amount of frost. You can help the ripening process, particularly if the summer has not been a good one, by using a high-potash fertilizer such as a tomato feed. Follow the manufacturer's instructions.

Plants in pots should be kept very dry during the winter, as this helps them survive the cold.

Climbers against walls can be protected by covering them with horticultural fleece, polythene bubble wrap, or a lean-to of wire netting that has been stuffed with straw or hurdles of reeds and propped up against the wall.

## HOT, DRY CONDITIONS

Hot, dry spots either outside or in south-facing, sun-baked greenhouses make good homes for Greek island compositions of vivid geraniums and intense bougainvilleas.

## CREATING A JUNGLE-EFFECT GREENHOUSE

Most of the large-leaved evergreen climbers need heat and humidity. The large, glossy leaves of *Philodendron scandens*, *Syngonium podophyllum*, *Dioscorea discolor*, *Epipremnum aureum*, and *Monstera deliciosa* (the Swiss cheese plant) will all give a tropical rain forest effect to a heated but shady greenhouse. These plants will thrive indoors because they do not need high light levels and, as a matter of fact, are often sold as houseplants. *Aristolochia elegans*, with its huge, slightly sinister, maroon and white marbled flowers, would also do well in these conditions and create a splendidly exotic effect.

Tropical plants like allamanda, lagenaria, luffa, manettia, nepenthes, granadilla, and jade vine all require warm, humid conditions and good light year-round.

Bougainvillea comes in a range of colors, including orange and pink, as well as this pretty rose red. Bougainvillea revels in full sun and a warm climate.

The jade vine, *Strongylodon macrobotrys*, is a fast-growing, twining climber that produces blue-green flowers in long, pendant spikes.

# Tropical and subtropical conditions

SOME OF THE MOST FLAMBOYANT and exciting climbers need really high temperatures in order to flourish. Others need humidity, too. It is important to choose the right plant for your conditions.

## TROPICAL PLANTS

A greenhouse needs to be kept at a minimum temperature of 60°F in order to successfully grow tropical climbers. Below are some examples of plants that will flourish in warm temperatures:

*Allamanda cathartica*
*Antigonon leptopus*
*Aristolochia elegans*
*Aristolochia gigantea*
*Bauhinia galpinii*
*Beaumontia grandiflora*
*Epipremnum aureum*
*Clytostoma callistegioides*
*Hoya bella*
*Ipomoea alba*
*Jasminum sambac*
*Mandevilla × amoena*
   'Alice du Pont'

*Mucuna bennettii*
*Passiflora alata*
*Passiflora coccinea*
*Passiflora racemosa*
*Petrea volubilis*
*Senecio macroglossus*
*Solandra maxima*
*Solanum wendlandii*
*Stephanotis floribunda*
*Stigmaphyllon ciliatum*
*Strongylodon macrobotrys*
*Thunbergia grandiflora*

## SUBTROPICAL PLANTS

Subtropical plants need a minimum temperature of 50°F. The following list suggests a range of plants that can be grown in subtropical conditions:

*Araujia sericifera*
*Bomarea caldasii*
*Bougainvillea spectabilis*
   and cvs
*Chorizema ilicifolium*
*Cissus antarctica*
*Cissus rhombifolia*
*Distictis buccinatoria*
*Gelsemium sempervirens*
*Gloriosa superba*
*Hardenbergia violacea*
*Hibbertia scandens*

*Hoya carnosa*
*Ipomoea indica*
*Ipomoea. purpurea*
*Ipomoea batatas*
*Kennedia sp.*
*Lonicera hildebrandiana*
*Macfadyena unguis-cati*
*Mandevilla laxa*
*Metrosideros sp.*
*Milletia megasperma*
*Mutisia ilicifolia*
*Pandorea pandorana*

*Pandorea jasminoides*
*Passiflora × allardii*
*Passiflora × belotii*
*Passiflora × caeruleoracemosa*
*Passiflora edulis*
*Passiflora ligularis*
*Passiflora manicata*
*Passiflora mollissima*
*Passiflora quadrangularis*
*Plumbago auriculata*
*Pyrostegia venusta*

*Gloriosa rothschildiana* grows from a tuber each spring and dies back in the fall. In warm climates it can be planted in the summer, but in temperate zones a pot culture is best.

## GREENHOUSE PESTS

As soon as you provide a warm place in winter, pests will find it and multiply, safe from their outdoor predators, and subsist on your precious plants. There are few really effective insecticides, so the answer is vigilance. The first few pests can generally be removed by hand. Large infestations are much more difficult to control.

## Ants

Ants build nests in pots and damage plant roots. Water the compost and the base of the greenhouse walls with an ant killer or ant barrier.

## Aphids

Greenflies and blackflies weaken plants and distort leaves by sucking their sap. As soon as you see any signs, squash them. There are several derris, pyrethrum, or soap–based insecticides on the market that will keep the numbers down. Grow *Tagetes patula* (French marigolds) in pots to attract hoverflies, the larvae of which eat aphids. Keep the house humid and well ventilated.

## Mealybugs

These insects are covered with a waxy white powder and white filaments. If you want to try biological control, the predator *Cryptolaemus montrouzierican* can be introduced in late spring. Before that, use a soap–based insecticide.

## Red Spider Mites

Signs of infestation are gray or yellowish mottling of leaves and very fine webs on the plants. Increase the humidity by spraying the surrounds and the undersides of the leaves with water frequently. Use biological control by introducing *Phytoseiulus persimilis* as soon as the daytime temperature in the greenhouse reaches 70°F.

## Scale Insects

Flat, brown or gray, round or oval scales appear on stems and the undersides of leaves. Like aphids, these are sap suckers. If there are only a few, these can be removed by scraping them off with a fingernail. Currently there are no chemical products on the market that deal with this problem.

## Vine Weevils

The larvae of vine weevils eat the roots of plants below the soil. Plants grow very slowly, then wilt and die. Biological control is available; nematodes are watered into the pots as soon as the compost temperature goes above 54°F. Vine weevil killers based on imidacloprid are now available and have been found effective.

## Whiteflies

Whiteflies cover leaves with a sticky honeydew and fly up in clouds from the plants when they are moved. Biological control, the parasitic wasp *Encarsia formosa*, is widely available, but the temperature in the greenhouse needs to have reached a minimum of 50°F. Under that, use sticky yellow traps or spray with soap–based insecticide or pyrethrum.

## Woodlice

These will eat roots and seedlings but mainly live on decaying material. Keep the greenhouse clear of dead leaves and plants.

# Hanging baskets and containers

HANGING BASKETS AND CONTAINERS are wonderful ways of adding splashes of color to a garden. Most of the plants used are tender annuals, like petunias and geraniums, but tender climbers are good alternatives and, with care, will last from season to season.

## Planting a hanging basket

Some smaller, tender climbers look very effective in hanging baskets. The long, arching or trailing stems look very graceful cascading down. The baskets can be moved around—in the warmest months they can hang outside in a sheltered, sunny spot and as the nights draw in and temperatures start to drop they can be brought into a sunny greenhouse or covered porch.

1 Select the largest hanging basket you can find. The larger they are, the easier they are to maintain. Line the basket with moss, bark, or fiber.

2 Line the basket with plastic sheeting, which will prevent the compost from drying out too quickly. Make drainage holes in the plastic sheeting (A).

3 Fill the container with good potting compost mixed with added slow-release fertilizer granules and a teaspoon or so of water-retaining gel granules.

4 Before planting, water the climbing plants you are going to use in the basket and leave for thirty minutes. Plant into the basket, packing well and watering again (B).

5 Mulch the surface with bark or lightweight aggregate to retain moisture.

A

B

## CARING FOR THE BASKET

Hanging baskets are essentially for short-lived displays. However, keeping the basket above 50°F and on the dry side in winter will help the plants. Judicious cutting back in winter is a good idea and the basket should be replanted with fresh compost and slow-release fertilizer in spring. Prune again in spring, to strong outward-facing buds in order to keep the plant in check. The baskets may need watering twice a day in the hottest season.

## TENDER CLIMBERS FOR HANGING BASKETS

| | |
|---|---|
| *Bougainvillea glabra* 'Harrissii' | *Cissus rhombifolia* |
| *Bougainvillea x buttiana* 'Rainbow Gold' | *Gelsemium sempervirens* |
| | *Hoya lanceolata bella* |
| *Chorizema* | *Maurandya barclaiana* |
| *Cissus antarctica* | *Pelargonium peltatum* |
| *Cissus striata* | *Senecio macroglossus* |
| | *Thunbergia alata* |

# Planting a Container

Many tropical or subtropical plants will grow happily in containers and can thus be grown in cooler regions, as the containers can be moved indoors in the coldest periods of the year. Deciduous or herbaceous plants can be stored in a cellar or garage but must be brought into the light as soon as the weather warms up.

1 Put a drainage layer of bricks or large stones about 4 in. deep at the bottom of the container (A). This can be covered with a sheet of fiberglass insulation material to prevent fine soil particles from washing through and impeding drainage.

2 Fill the container with five parts John Innes No. 3 potting compost mixed with one part sand and gravel.

3 This is the point at which to add any supports, canes, or pieces of trellis for the plants to grow up.

4 As with hanging baskets, water the climbers in their pots before you plant them. Pack them in well, water again, and mulch the surface with bark, gravel, or large pebbles (B).

A

B

## CHOOSING PLANTS

The following plants do well in containers:

| | |
|---|---|
| Allamanda cathartica | Manettia bicolor |
| Bomarea caldasii | Mandevilla × amoena 'Alice |
| Bougainvillea 'Los Banos | du Pont' |
| Beauty' | Mandevilla splendens |
| Bougainvillea 'Temple Fire' | Sollya heterophylla |
| Hibbertia scandens | Stephanotis floribunda |

## CONTAINER CARE

Containers need to be watered regularly, particularly in hot weather, when they should be watered twice a day. A liquid feed, prepared according to the manufacturer's instructions and given weekly, is also advantageous for the plants and will help them to flourish. A yearly top dressing, replacing the top 1 in. of compost in the container with fresh compost, is recommended.

# PLANT DIRECTORY

## CLIMATE ZONES

All of the plants listed in the Plant Directory are given climate zones, which indicates the temperature range they will thrive in.

| Climate Zone | Average Minimum Temperature |
|---|---|
| Zone 1 | −50°F |
| Zone 2 | −50° to −40°F |
| Zone 3 | −40° to −30°F |
| Zone 4 | −30° to −20°F |
| Zone 5 | −20° to −10°F |
| Zone 6 | −10° to 0°F |
| Zone 7 | 0° to 10°F |
| Zone 8 | 10° to 20°F |
| Zone 9 | 20° to 30°F |
| Zone 10 | 30° to 40°F |
| Zone 11 | over 40°F |

## A

*Aconitum hemsleyanum* (Climbing monkshood) has relatively large mauve-blue flowers. Some clones have better color than others, so buy it in flower if you can (Zone 8).

*Actinidia arguta* has satiny green leaves and small, fragrant flowers and will grow to 65 ft. (Zone 4). *A. chinensis*, (Chinese gooseberry or kiwi fruit) will grow to 33 ft. or more. The stems and leaves are covered with noticeable red hairs. The heart-shaped leaves can be 6–8 in. long. The white flowers are followed by large, oval fruits. *A. kolomikta* has long leaves, the upper sections often creamy-white and pink. *A. melanandra* has lance-shaped leaves on long pink stalks and white flowers, followed by egg-shaped fruits (Zone 5).

*Adlumia fungosa* (Climbing fumitory) has fernlike leaves and drooping, pinkish-white flowers similar to those of a dicentra (Zone 8).

*Akebia quinata* (Chocolate vine) is a vigorous twiner with maroon-purple, scented flowers in spring and pretty, five-leafleted leaves (Zone 4). *A. trifoliata* has three-lobed leaves, small flowers, and larger fruits. *A. × pentaphylla* is a hybrid between them.

*Allamanda cathartica* (Golden Trumpet) is a scrambling shrub that bears its rich yellow flowers in clusters in summer and fall. Thrives in full sun and plenty of warmth; also wind tolerant (Zone 10).

*Ampelopsis glandulosa brevipedunculata* is a vigorous, deciduous tendril climber with lobed, dark green leaves and bright blue berries (Zone 4). *A. g .b.* 'Elegans' has pink and white variegated leaves but is frost-tender and less vigorous. *A. megalophylla* has the longest leaves of all hardy plants, and black berries (Zone 6).

*Anredera cordifolia* (Mignonette Vine) has highly scented, tiny white flowers in racemes in the fall (Zone 9).

*Apios americana* (Potato bean) is a slender climber with pinnate leaves that flowers in late summer/early fall, with clusters of pea-shaped flowers in a deep brown-red (Zone 3).

*Araujia sericifera* (Cruel Plant) traps moths with its sticky pollen at night. It has star-shaped white flowers from late spring to late fall (Zone 9).

*Aristolochia macrophylla* (Dutchman's Pipe) is a twining plant with yellowish-green, bent tubular flowers with a purple-brown border, but these are often hidden by the heart-shaped leaves that get larger as they age (Zone 4).

*Asteranthera ovata* has small, crinkled leaves and large, red trumpet flowers from summer onward (Zones 8–9).

## B

*Beaumontia grandiflora* (Easter lily vine) has scented, white, bell-shaped flowers, 5 in. long, born in profusion, displayed against large, glossy, dark green leaves (Zone 9).

*Berberidopsis corallina* (Coral plant) has rich, evergreen leaves and hanging clusters of crimson, globular flowers (Zones 8–9).

*Billardiera longiflora* (Apple Berry) is a slender climber with narrow leaves, greenish-yellow bells, followed by blue berries (Zones 8–9).

*Bomarea caldasii* has hanging tubular flowers, like an alstromeria, in clusters, that vary from yellow to orange and red (Zones 8–9).

*Bougainvillea glabra* has woody stems with thorns and brilliantly colored bracts of cyclamen purple surrounding small white flowers (Zone 9). Most of the cultivars available are *B. g.* crosses, *B. × buttiana* or varieties of *B. spectabilis*, and the bracts vary in color. There are white, orange, scarlet, puce, and deep red varieties.

## C

*Campsis grandiflora* has ashlike pinnate leaves and showy orange trumpet flowers with red veins (Zone 7). *C. radicans* has orange-tubed, red-petaled flowers and is more vigorous (Zone 4); while *C. × tagliabuana* 'Madame Galen' has salmon-red trumpets, freely borne (Zone 4).

*Celastrus orbiculatus* (Oriental bittersweet, Staff vine) is an untidy twining plant with rounded leaves but colorful in the fall with red seeds in yellow-lined seed cases and a good yellow leaf color (Zone 4). *C. scandens* (American bittersweet) is less vigorous (Zone 2).

*Chorizema cordatum* (Australian flame pea) is a perennial climber with bunches of small pea flowers in orange, with a purple keel (Zones 8–9). *C. ilicifolium* (Holly flame pea) has small, hollylike leaves and pink and orange flowers (Zones 8–9).

*Cissus antarctica* (Kangaroo vine) is a foliage climber, with rich green, oval, toothed leaves (Zones 9–10). *C. rhombifolia* (Grape ivy) is similar but with trifoliate leaves (Zones 9–10).

*Clematis:*
*Clematis* species and cultivars are hardy, slender plants that climb by using their leaf stalk tendrils. The flowers are

usually made up of four petal-like sepals, which sometimes form a bell shape but are often flat, like a saucer. *C. aethusifolia* has ferny leaves and pale yellow bellflowers on a delicate plant (Zone 4).

*C. alpina* has pendulous, lantern-shaped flowers in blue, white, or pink in late spring (Zone 5). 'Francis Rivis' is deep blue. 'Ruby' is red. 'Helsingborg' is deep purple.

*C. armandii* is evergreen with white, scented flowers in spring (Zone 7).

*C. cirrhosa* will climb to 12 ft., flowering in winter with creamy-white bells (Zone 7). *C. c. balearica* 'Freckles' has red spots inside.

*C. flammula* has wiry stems and long panicles of scented white flowers in late summer and the fall (Zone 6).

*C. florida* 'Sieboldii' has white flowers with a center of deep purple petaloid stamens (Zone 6).

*C. indivisa* is evergreen, with glossy leaves and large white flowers (Zone 8).

*C. macropetala* (Zone 5); As the name indicates, the bell-shaped blue, pink, or white flowers on these species are semidouble, the centers full of small, narrow petals. 'Markhams Pink' has mauve-pink flowers. 'Maidwell Hall' is deep blue.

*C. montana* (Zone 5); White or pink four-petaled flowers smother this very vigorous plant in late spring/early summer every year. *C. m. grandiflora* has large white flowers. *C. m. var. rubens* has pink flowers. *C. m. var. r.* 'Tetrarose' has larger pink flowers. *C. m. var. r.* 'Freda' has deep cherry-pink flowers and bronze foliage.

*C. orientalis* has pretty yellow, thick-petaled flowers followed by fluffy seedheads in late summer and fall (Zone 6). *C. o.* 'Bill Mackenzie' has larger flowers.

*C. rehderiana* has cowslip-scented, small bellflowers of primrose yellow in late summer (Zone 6).

*C. terniflora* has starlike white flowers in profusion from late summer to midfall.

*C. × cartmanii* 'Moonbeam' grows to only 3 ft. and has greenish-cream flowers in late spring/early summer.

*C. × triternata* 'Rubromarginata' has clusters of strongly scented, white flowers with deep pink margins from midsummer to early fall (Zone 5).

*Clematis × vedrariensis* 'Rosea' is similar to *C. m. var. rubens* except that it has hairs

on the leaves. The variety 'Hidcote' has small, deeper pink flowers.

*Viticellas* and their hybrids and cultivars are small, late-flowering clematises (Zone 4):
'Etoile Violette'–violet.
'Kermesina'–deep red, prolific.
'Madame Julia Correvon'–wine-red with yellow anthers.
'Minuet'–white with reddish-mauve edges.
'Purpurea Plena Elegans'–purple, double flowers.
'Venosa Violacea'–white with violet edges.

Large-flowered hybrids:
'Barbara Jackman'–mauve with a petunia red bar.
'Beauty of Worcester'–violet blue.
'Belle of Woking'–double, silver-mauve.
'Daniel Deronda'–large, deep violet blue, semidouble and single flowers.
'Dr Ruppel'–deep rose pink with a deeper bar.
'Duchess of Edinburgh'–white double flowers.
'Ernest Markham'–purple-red.
'Gravetye Beauty'–deep, rich red, pitcher-shaped flowers.
'Hagley Hybrid'–shell pink.
'Huldine'–white petals with mauve reverse.
'Lasurstern'–very large lavender-blue flowers.
'Mme Baron Veillard'–bright lilac pink.
'Marie Boisselot'–pure white, long-flowering.
'Nelly Moser'–large flowers, pale mauve with a pink stripe.
'Niobe'–deep red, free-flowering for a long season.
'Perle d'Azur'–the truest blue.
'Scartho Gem'–bright pink with a deeper bar.
'Sylvia Denney'–white with yellow stamens.
'The President'–purple blue, free-flowering, and compact.
'The Princess of Wales'–bright pink, hanging, tulip-shaped flowers.
'Ville de Lyon'–bright crimson red.
'William Kennett'–mid-blue.

*Clianthus puniceus* (Parrot's beak or Lobster claw) has brilliant scarlet flowers (one can also find coral-pink or white) are borne in clusters of between six and fifteen blooms each up to 3 in. long and attractive foliage (Zone 8).

*Cobaea scandens* (Cup and saucer vine) is a fast-growing perennial with purple bellflowers; there is also a pale green form, sold as 'Alba'. It climbs by leaf tendrils and will flower the first year from seed, so it can be used as an annual (Zone 9).

*Codonopsis convolvulacea* is a slender climber that may reach 6 ft. with open clusters of lilac-blue bellflowers in late summer (Zone 8).

## D

*Decumaria barbara* is a climbing hydrangea, deciduous or semievergreen, with clusters of white, scented flowers, but without the showy bracts of other climbing hydrangeas (Zone 7). *D. sinensis* is evergreen but less tolerant of cold (Zone 8).

*Dicentra scandens* (Zone 5) has racemes of pendant yellow, slightly heart-shaped flowers, tipped with pink or light purple and light, ferny foliage. *D. macrocapnos* has similar flowers but is more vigorous.

*Dichelostemma volubile* is a half-hardy perennial twiner with long, allium-like leaves and 3-ft. flowering stems with pink flowers (Zone 8).

*Distictis buccinatoria* (Mexican Blood Flower) has deep rose-crimson tubular flowers, is orange-yellow inside, and has handsome, glossy dark green leaves. It climbs by tendrils that have clinging disks (Zone 9).

## E

*Eccremocarpus scaber* (Chilean glory flower) has orange-red tubular flowers and climbs using lots of tiny tendrils (Zones 8–9). *E. s. carmineus* is red; *E. s. aureus*, yellow; and *E. s. roseus*, pink.

*Ercilla volubilis* is an evergreen root climber with deep green leaves, with paler veins and spikes of whitish-pink flowers in spring (Zones 8–9).

*Euonymus fortunei* is a scandent shrub with handsome, glossy, evergreen leaves (Zone 5). *E. fortunei* 'Silver Queen' has white variegations, *E. f.* 'Emerald 'n' Gold' has bright yellow variegation. *E. f. var. radicans* is a particularly good climbing variety, but all climb in the right situation.

## F

*Fallopia baldschuanica* (Russian vine or "mile-a-minute") is a deciduous twiner with oval leaves and panicles of small white flowers in late summer (Zone 4).

× *Fatshedera lizei* (Tree ivy) is a scrambling shrub, a cross between ivy and fatsia, which has large, deeply lobed, glossy evergreen leaves (Zone 7).

## G

*Gloriosa superba* (Glory Lily) grows from a tuber and produces slender stems and leaves with long points that taper into a tendril and yellow (aging to red) Turk's cap, lily-shaped flowers. *G. rothschildiana* is similar (Zone 9).

## H

*Hardenbergia violacea* (Zone 9), the vine lilac or false sarsparilla, has violet blue pea flowers in long racemes. It will climb to 6 ft. and cultivars are available in white and pink, as well as violet.

*Hedera canariensis* 'Ravensholst' is a large-leafed ivy. Leaves can be up to 8 in. long (Zones 7–8).
*H. colchica* (Persian Ivy) has heart-shaped leaves up to 8 in. long (Zone 5).
*H. c.* 'Dentata' has toothed edges.
*H. c.* 'Dentata Variegata' and *H. c.* 'Sulphur Heart' (or 'Paddy's Pride') are variegated forms.
*H. helix* (Common ivy) is a self-clinging climber with dark green leaves and a variable number of lobes (Zone 5).
*H. h.* 'Atropurpurea' has pale veins and turns purple in the fall.
*H. h.* 'Chrysophylla' has green and yellow leaves on the same plant.
*H. h.* 'Glymii' leaves turn purple in cold.
*H. h.* 'Goldchild', yellow variegations.
*H. h.* 'Green Ripple' has deep-cut leaves.
*H. h.* 'Ivalace' has small, dark, wavy leaves.
*H. h.* 'Lemon Swirl', white variegations.
*H. h.* 'Little Diamond', white variegations.
*H. h.* 'Oro di Bogliasco', (or 'Goldheart'), yellow centers.
*H. h.* 'Parsley Crested', crimped margins.
*H. h.* 'Pink and Curly' has crinkled edges with pink on the back.
*H. h.* 'Sagittifoli', arrow-shaped leaves.
*H. h.* var. *baltica* is exceptionally hardy.
*H. hibernica* (Irish ivy) has broad leaves and is a strong grower.
*H. h.* 'Digitata' has five or seven narrow lobes.

*Hibbertia scandens* (Gold guinea plant or Snake vine) is a near hardy, twining evergreen with wonderful, rich yellow flowers, 2 in. across (Zone 9).

*Holboellia coriacea* has thick, shiny leaves and purple-green male and larger, greenish-white female flowers on the plant at the same time in late spring (Zone 7). *H. latifolia* is vigorous with white flowers flushed with purple in late spring (Zone 8).

*Humulus lupulus* 'Aureus' (Zone 6), the golden hop, is an herbaceous twiner with toothed, yellowish leaves with three or five lobes.

*Hydrangea anomala* subsp. *petiolaris*, (Climbing hydrangea) has small white flowers surrounded by whitish bracts in broad corymbs in midsummer (Zone 4). *H. seemannii* is evergreen with dark, leathery leaves and white flowers (Zone 8).

## I

*Ipomoeas* (Bindweeds or Convolvulus) are fast-growing, twining plants. Some of them can become weeds (Zone 9). *I. alba* (Moonflower) is a herbaceous climber with white trumpets 5 in. long (Zones 9–10). *I. batatas* 'Blackie' has deep red leaves and stems, with light purple trumpet flowers (Zone 9). *I. coccinea* is red (Zone 5). *I. indica* is a rich purple. *I. lobata*, Mina, has small racemes of scarlet flowers fading to white. *I. nil* will grow to 16 ft. in a season (Zone 9). Seeds are available for 'Flying Saucers', blue and white, or 'Scarlet O'Hara', red. *I. purpurea* has many cultivars in white, pink, and scarlet (Zone 5). *I. quamoclit* has small red flowers and feathery leaves. *I. tricolor* 'Heavenly Blue' (Morning glory) has large, sky-blue flowers (Zone 5).

## J

*Jasminum azoricum* is a semitwining evergreen with fragrant white flowers, purple in bloom (Zone 9). *J. beesianum* has small red flowers with rolled petals (Zone 6). *J. nudiflorum* (Winter jasmine) is a scrambler with yellow flowers in winter (Zone 5). *J. officinale* (Common jasmine) is vigorous with white flowers and is very fragrant (Zones 7–8). *J. polyanthum* has profuse pink flowers and is even more fragrant than the above (Zone 9). *J. sambac* (Arabian jasmine) has very fragrant, waxy white jasmine flowers and attractive evergreen foliage (Zone 10). *J. × stephanense* is similar to *J. officinale* but with light pink flowers (Zones 7–8).

## K

*Kadsura japonica* is a twining evergreen with creamy yellow flowers from leaf axils between midsummer and fall, followed by red fruits (Zone 8).

*Kennedia coccinea* (Coral pea) has umbels of between three and twelve scarlet pea flowers (Zone 9). *K. nigricans* (Black coral pea) has flowers of yellow and dark brown-purple (Zone 9). *K. rubicunda* (Dusky coral pea) has coral-red flowers in small trusses (Zone 9).

## L

*Lapageria rosea* (Chilean bellflower) is a twining evergreen with magnificent large, waxy textured, bell-shaped flowers in white or pink (Zones 8–9).

*Lardizabala biternata* is an evergreen twiner with glossy compound leaves and male and female chocolate-purple flowers, followed by purple fruits (Zone 9).

*Lathyrus chloranthus* has acid yellow pea flowers (Zone 7). *L. grandiflorus* (Everlasting pea) has red and pinkish-purple flowers (Zone 6). *L. latifolius* (Perennial sweet pea) has pinkish-purple flowers (Zone 5). *L. l.* 'Albus' has white flowers and *L. l.* 'Rosa Perle' is pink. *L. nervosus* 'Lord Anson's Blue Pea' is small with light blue flowers (Zone 7). *L. odoratus* (Sweet pea) has is found in white, pale yellow, mauve, pink, purple, and red (Zone 3).

*Lonicera × brownii* (Zones 6–7) Scarlet Trumpet Honeysuckle, red fragrant flowers and oval blue-green leaves. 'Dropmore Scarlet' has a longer flowering season. *L. etrusca* 'Superba' (Zone 7) has creamy-yellow flowers in late summer. *L. × heckrottii* (Zone 5) is a scrambler with clusters of yellow flowers, red in bud. *L. henryi* (Zone 5) flowers in midsummer with terminal clusters of small, yellow flowers flushed with reddish purple. *L. hildebrandiana* (Zone 9) is the largest honeysuckle with slender flowers 5–7 in. long. *L. × italica* (Zone 5), free-flowering with clusters of highly scented, yellow flowers flushed with red-purple in summer.

*L. japonica* (Zones 6–8) is a fast-growing evergreen honeysuckle. 'Aureoreticulata' has green leaves netted with yellow; the flowers are insignificant. *L .j.* 'Halliana' and *L. j.* 'Hall's Prolific' have bright green leaves and yellow, highly scented flowers. *L. periclymenum* (Zone 4), the common honeysuckle or woodbine, has long, tubed flowers, dark purple on the outside and pale pink within. 'Belgica' flowers in midsummer. 'Graham Thomas' has white flowers aging to yellow. 'Serotina', or 'Late Dutch', flowers in late summer. *L. sempervirens sulphurea* (Zone 7), a yellow-flowering form of the coral honeysuckle with tubular flowers in drooping spikes and a long flowering period. *L. similis var. delavayi* (Zone 7) is evergreen with large leaves and white, strongly scented, tubular flowers over a long period. *L. × tellmanniana* (Zone 6) has bright yellow flowers flushed with orange-red. *L. tragophylla* (Zone 6) has large leaves and flowers of bright yellow up to 3½ in. long.

*Lophospermum erubescens* (Zones 8–9), perennial twining snapdragons, often called Asarina or Maurandya, with typical snapdragon flowers in rose pink. Treat as an annual in cool areas. *L. scandens* has lavender flowers.

*Lycium chinense* (Zone 6), a deciduous scrambler with small purple flowers, followed by a profusion of scarlet berries in the fall.

## M

*Macfadyena unguis-cati* (Zones 9–10), 'Cat's claw vine', is an evergreen tendril climber, grown for its yellow, foxglove-like flowers.

*Mandevilla laxa* (Zone 9), the Chilean jasmine, has highly perfumed, white, funnel-shaped flowers. The foliage is not exciting and it is grown for its perfume. *M. × amoena* 'Alice du Pont' has abundant rose-pink flowers. *M. splendens* (Zones 9–10), large, deep pink flowers.

*Maurandella antirrhiniflora* (Zones 8–9) is a slender-stemmed climber with violet-purple snapdragon flowers. Grow as an annual.

*Maurandya barclayana* (Zones 8–9) is a woody-based climbing snapdragon with flowers that vary from white and pink to deep purple.

*Menispermum canadense* (Zone 4), Moonseed. Woody twiner with circular leaves and blue-black berries in October to November.

*Merremia tuberosa* (Zone 9), 'Wood Rose', 'Yellow Morning Glory'. Fast-growing evergreen with with funnel-shaped yellow flowers, with a deeper colored throat in summer.

*Metrosideros carmineus* (Zone 9), a self-clinging evergreen with brilliant scarlet flowers.

*Milletia megasperma* (Zone 9), the evergreen wisteria, has racemes of deep indigo flowers and leathery leaves darker than the deciduous species.

*Mitraria coccinea* (Zone 8), evergreen scrambler with scarlet, tubular flowers and small, dark green leaves.

*Mucuna pruriens* (Zone 8), the velvet bean, or Florida bean, it has 12-in. racemes of deep purple or purple-black pea flowers.

*Muehlenbeckia complexa* (Zone 7), dark purple, wiry stems have dark green leaves; tiny star-shaped flowers are followed by small white berries.

*Mutisia decurrens* (Zone 8) has showy, bright orange daisy flowers. *M. oligodon* (Zone 8) has orange-pink flowers, while those of *M. ilicifolia* (Zone 9) are pink or mauve. It has leathery, holly-shaped leaves.

## P

*Paederia scandens* (Zone 7) is a hardy, deciduous twiner with dark green leaves and creamy, tubular flowers with purple throats. *P. foetida* is lilac; *P. tomentosa*, rose-purple.

*Pandorea jasminoides* (Zone 9), 'Bower of Beauty', has shiny evergreen foliage and foxglove-like flowers in pale pink with a red throat. *P. pandorana*, the wonga-wonga vine, has smaller cream flowers splashed with red or purple.

*Parthenocissus henryana* (Zone 8), the Chinese Virginia creeper, has conspicuously white-veined leaves that turn red in the fall. Insignificant flowers are sometimes followed by blue-black berries.

*P. quinquefolia* (Zone 3), Virginia creeper. The leaves made up of five leaflets turn scarlet in the fall.

*P. tricuspidata* (Zone 4) is often also called the Virginia creeper. It has maplelike leaves with three lobes. *P. tricuspidata* 'Lowii' has leaves that are cut and crimped at the edges.

*Passiflora alata* (Zone 9), the flowers are 4–5 in. across with dark crimson flowers and hanging filaments striped white and violet.
*P.* 'Allardii' (Zone 9) has large, scented, pink, white, and blue flowers.
*P. × belotii* (Zone 9), fragrant flowers, 5 in. across in white, pink, and blue.
*P. caerulea* (Zones 8–9), common or blue passionflower, is almost hardy in the U.K. Deeply cut, dark green leaves and 2½ to 4-in.-wide flowers with white sepals and a blue or purple-and-white banded corona. *P .c.* 'Constance Elliott' (Zones 8–9) is pure white.
*P. × caeruleoracemosa* (Zone 9) has three-lobed leaves and soft purple flowers.
*P. coccinea* (Zone 9) has oval leaves and showy scarlet flowers 3–4 in. across.
*P. edulis* (Zone 9), purple pranadilla, true passion fruit, has green and white flowers followed by edible purple fruits.
*P. ligularis* (Zone 9), the sweet granadilla, has large white and purple flowers from June to September, followed by sweet, edible fruit.
*P. manicata* (Zone 9) has large, bright scarlet and purple flowers from May to October, and edible fruit.
*P. mollissina* (Zone 9), the banana passionflower, has pink flowers and banana-shaped, edible fruit.
*P. quadrangularis* (Zones 9–10), the giant granadilla, has large leaves and fragrant, bowl-shaped flowers with red petals and purple and white banded filaments.
*P. racemosa* (Zone 9) has leathery leaves and long, almost leafless, sprays of bright red flowers.

*Pelargonium peltatum* (Zone 9), the ivy-leaved geranium, a trailing plant with fleshy leaves and, in the species, carmine-red flowers. The cascade pelargoniums, such as 'Roi de Balcons', derive from this.

*Periploca graeca* (Zones 7–8), the common silk vine, a deciduous twiner with brownish, purple-petaled flowers and seeds with silky hairs.

*Petrea volubilis* (Zones 9–10), the purple wreath, has racemes of starry flowers with violet petals and lilac sepals in spring.

*Pileostegia viburnoides* (Zone 7) is a root climber with long, oval leaves and flattened heads of creamy white flowers in the fall.

*Plumbago auriculata* (Zone 9), cape leadwort, is a vigorous scrambler with sky-blue flowers a little like primroses.

*Pueraria lobata* (Zones 7–8), the kudzu vine, is a leguminous perennial with trifoliate leaves and racemes of fragrant, red-purple pea flowers in late summer.

*Pyrostegia venusta* (Zone 9–10), the flame vine, a vigorous tendril climber with clusters of tubular flowers in a rich golden-orange.

## R

*Rhodochiton atrosanguineus* (Zone 9) is an evergreen perennial that can be grown as an annual. It has long, tubular, dark purple flowers with a pagoda top in reddish-purple.

*Rosa* species:
*Rosa banksiae* (Zones 8–9), the Banksian rose. *R. b.* 'Lutea' the yellow Banksian rose, is most frequently grown and has violet, scented, small, double yellow flowers in clusters in spring.
*R brunonii* (Zone 8), the Himalayan musk rose, has single white flowers in clusters and stems that grow to between 15 and 35 ft. long. *R. b.* 'La Mortola' is an even stronger grower.
*R canina* (Zone 4), the dog rose or common brier, has single pink flowers and can scramble 15 ft. into a tree.
*R filipes* 'Kiftsgate' (Zone 6) is a robust and extremely vigorous rose with small cream flowers in large trusses, followed by small hips.
*R mulligani* is less vigorous than *R filipes*, and has single, pure white flowers in small clusters.
*R setigera* (Zone 5), the prairie rose, is another scrambler with flowers that vary from crimson to white.
*R wichurana* (Zones 6–7) has leathery evergreen leaves and trusses of small white flowers in late summer.

*Rosa* cultivars:
'Alberic Barbier', a rambler with lustrous foliage and clusters of double, cream flowers.
'Alister Stella Gray', climber with noisette, 3-in. flowers of rich yellow.
'Bobbie James' is a giant rambler with large clusters of creamy-white, semidouble flowers.
'Champney's Pink Cluster', a repeat-flowering climber with noisette flowers, pink flushed with deeper pink.
'Chewpixel', Open Arms, a miniature rambler with small, semidouble pink flowers throughout the summer.
'Chewizz', Warm Welcome, a miniature climber with orange flowers all summer.
'Climbing Cécile Brunner', a vigorous climber with perfect shell-pink blooms.
'Climbing Iceberg', medium-sized, pure white flowers over a long period.
'Crown Princess Margareta', a small climber with neat rosette flowers of apricot-orange.
'Desprez a Fleurs Jaunes', a very old climber with flat, many-petaled warm yellow flowers shaded with peachy pink.
'Dr. W. Van Fleet', a rambler with soft pink flowers and glossy foliage.
'Easlea's Golden Rambler' is a rich yellow and blooms once.
'Evangeline', a rambler with clusters of soft, pinkish-white flowers late in the season.
'Excelsa', Red Dorothy Perkins, has large trusses of light crimson flowers and very dark green leaves.
'Félicité Perpétue', a rambler with neat foliage and double, creamy white pom-pom flowers from pink buds.
'Gertrude Jekyll', neat buds expand into large, rich pink rosettes.
'Guinee', a climber with highly scented and the darkest crimson flowers of any rose.
'Handel' is a modern climber with cream flowers edged with rose-pink.
'Lawrence Johnson', a strong-growing climber with canary yellow flowers once in the season.
'Little Rambler' has small double flowers of light pink that pale as they age. Repeat flowering.
'Madame Alfred Carrière', hardy, noisette-flowered climber with white flowers tinted with soft pink.
'Madame Grégoire Staechelin', Spanish Beauty, large semidouble flowers in glowing pink, in clusters. Flowers once.
'Maigold', bronze-yellow, semidouble flowers, flowers once early in season.
'Mermaid', large, single canary yellow flowers over the summer.

'Paul's Himalayan Musk', rambler with open sprays of blush-pink rosette flowers in profusion.
'Paul's Scarlet Climber', large clusters of brilliant scarlet flowers.
'Phyllis Bide', a repeat-flowering rambler, small yellow flowers flushed with pink.
'Rambling Rector', a strong climber with creamy flowers that open white, showing yellow stamens, followed by red hips.
'Sombreuil', a climber with flat, quartered flowers of white tinged with flesh-pink.
'Treasure Trove', a vigorous rambler with apricot-pink flowers.
'Veilchenblau', an almost thornless rambler with small, semidouble flowers that start purple and age to lilac.
'Wedding Day', a prolific rambler with yellow buds that open to cream and then turn white.
'White Cockade', an upright climber, small glossy leaves and double pure white flowers.
'Zéphirine Drouhin', deep pink roses produced over a long period and in profusion. Thornless.

*Rubus flagelliflorus* (Zone 7), a graceful scrambler with white-felted stems and shiny black fruits.
*R fruticosus laciniatus* 'Oregon Thornless', the thornless blackberry (Zone 4).
*R. f. l.* 'Parsley Leaved', decorative ferny leaves and edible black fruits.
*R ichangensis* (Zone 6), semievergreen, heart-shaped leaves, panicles of white flowers, and edible fruits. *R irenaeus* has large round leaves, small white flowers, followed by large red fruits. *R lineatus* (Zone 8), semievergreen with white-veined leaves like a horse chestnut, small fruit, and flowers. *R phoenicolasius* (Zone 5), the Japanese wineberry; red-bristled stems, light green leaves with white undersides, flowers encased by red-haired sepals, conical red edible fruits. *R ulmifolius* 'Bellidiflorus' (Zone 4), small, pink pom-pom flowers on this blackberry relation.

## S

*Schisandra chinensis* (Zone 5), woody-stemmed twiner with white or pale pink flowers borne in clusters in late spring. *S. rubriflora* (Zone 8) has small crimson flowers and red fruits. *S. sphenanthera* (Zone 7) has terra-cotta colored flowers in early summer.

*Schizophragma hydrangeoides* (Zone 5) is a self-clinging hydrangea with dark, heart-shaped leaves and cream flowers in lacy clusters surrounded by elegant bracts. *S. integrifolium* (Zone 7) is similar but has larger flower heads.

*Senecio macroglossus* (Zone 9), Cape ivy or wax vine. Thick glossy leaves and white daisy flowers. *S. m.* 'Variegatus' has yellow variegations.

*Smilax aspera* (Zone 7), rough bindweed, thorny, herbaceous, perennial climber with pale, glossy leaves, small scented flowers, and glossy red berries later. *S. rotundifolia* (Zone 4), horse brier, glossy heart-shaped leaves, yellow green flowers in summer followed by black berries covered with a white patina.

*Solanum crispum* 'Glasnevin' (Zone 8), blue-purple potato flowers on a scrambling, semiwoody shrub. Long flowering, semievergreen. *S. dulcamara* 'Variegatum' (Zone 4), variegated woody nightshade. Trailing perennial with poisonous red berries. *S. jasminoides* 'Album' (Zones 8-9), potato vine, is a true climber with twining leaf stalks. Pure white potato flowers from July to fall. *S. wendlandii* (Zone 9), giant Costa Rican potato vine, evergreen, climbs using sharp hooks. Lavender blue flowers, 2½ in. across in large bunches.

*Sollya heterophylla* (Zone 9), the Australian bluebell, is a perennial with pale green lanceolate leaves and sky-blue, bell-shaped flowers, ½ in. long.

*Stauntonia hexaphylla*, with dark glossy leaves and small clusters of white, fragrant flowers in spring, is another example of a very slightly tender plant that is well worth trying. In a good year, it even produces purple-red fruits.

*Stephanotis floribunda* (Zone 10), the wax flower, a twining plant that has waxy, pure white flowers and shiny evergreen leaves.

## T

*Teucrium fruticans* (Zone 9), a scrambling shrub with oval, gray-green leaves and small-lipped blue flowers on white stems, June to September.

*Thladiantha dubia* (Zone 8), a herbaceous perennial, growing to 15 ft. Heart-shaped leaves and bright yellow bell-shaped flowers. It is a member of the cucumber family.

*Thunbergia alata* (Zone 5), black-eyed Susan. Annual twiner with 2-in.-wide flowers with chocolate-brown centers. Colors range from white through yellow to orange. *T. grandiflora*, (Zones 9-10, or Zone 6 as an annual), the blue trumpet vine or blue skyflower, a vigorous, woody-stemmed climber with large blue flowers. *T. gregorii* (Zone 9, Zone 5 as an annual) has 2-in.-wide flowers of bright orange. *T. mysorensis* (Zones 9-10) has long racemes of golden flowers with brownish-red to purple tubes.

*Trachelospermum asiaticum* (Zone 9), the star jasmine, has glossy, dark green leaves in opposite pairs and small clusters of jasmine-like, scented white flowers. *T. jasminoides* (Zone 9) is a taller, better plant but needs more support and is less hardy. The leaves of *T. j.* 'Variegatum' have white edges.

*Tripterygium regelii* (Zone 4) grows to about 18 ft. It has handsome oval leaves about 6 in. long. In late summer, panicles of small white flowers are followed by greenish fruits with three wings.

*Tropaeolum azureum* (Zone 9) is a slender trailer with blue flowers shaped like a mimulus and slenderly lobed leaves. *T. majus* (Zone 5) is the annual nasturtium, and is available as seed in yellows, oranges, and reds. *T. peregrinum* (Zone 5), the canary creeper, grows to about 5 ft. and has small, yellow fringed flowers. *T. speciosum* (Zone 8), the flame vine, has vivid red flowers followed by deep blue fruits contrasting with purplish bracts. *T. tricolorum* (Zones 8-9), which grows to about 4 ft., has striking orange or yellow flowers from red-orange, black-tipped calyces. *T. tuberosum* (Zone 8, but the tubers can be replanted annually), of which the most widely available form is *T. tuberosum* var. *lineamaculatum* 'Ken Aslet', which has blue-green leaves and long-spurred, orange-red flowers.

*Tweedia caerulea* (Zone 9) is a small perennial twiner that grows to about 3 ft. with narrow, oblong, gray leaves and clusters of turquoise-blue flowers.

## V

*Vinca major* (Zone 7), the greater periwinkle, has shiny, rich green leaves and blue flowers. It will scramble through a shrub.

*Vitis amurensis* (Zone 4) is similar to the grapevine and has broad leaves that color to red and purple in the fall. *V.* 'Brant' (Zone 4) has leaves that turn bronze-red and purple in the fall. *V. coignetiae* (Zone 5) will grow to 60 ft. and has large 6-12 in. leaves that turn scarlet and apricot in the fall. *V. davidii* (Zone 6) has bristly stems and heart-shaped leaves that turn crimson in the fall. The small black grapes are edible. *V. flexuosa*, has small, bronze-green, shiny leaves, fluffy flowers, and a good fall color. *V. riparia* (Zone 2), the riverbank grape, has heart-shaped leaves and exceptional fall color. *V. labrusca* 'Concord' (Zone 5), the fox grape. It has thick, textured leaves and very good fruit. *V. parvifolia* (Zone 5) syn. *V. thunbergii* (Zone 6) is less vigorous; the leaves are brown-felted underneath and turn scarlet in the fall. *V. vinifera* (Zone 6), the grapevine, is deciduous. *V. v.* 'Ciotat' has finely dissected leaves. *V. v.* 'Purpurea' has claret-red leaves when young, which turn to red-purple as they age.

## W

*Wisteria:*
The wisterias are vigorous, woody twining plants that have pinnate leaves like an ash and pendant racemes of pea flowers, like a laburnum, followed by beanlike seed pods.
*Wisteria brachybotrys* (syn. *W. venusta*) (Zone 5) has chunky racemes of white flowers about 4-6 in. long.
*W. floribunda* 'Alba' (Zone 4), the Japanese wisteria, has racemes of white flowers that can be over 3 ft. in length.
*W. f.* 'Multijuga' has lilac-blue flowers.
*W. sinensis* (Zone 5), the Chinese wisteria, has shorter racemes of mauve to deep lilac flowers, between 5 to 10 in. long.
*W. s.* 'Prolific' is very vigorous.

## Suppliers

Ace Hardware
2200 Kensington Ct.
Oak Brook, IL 60523-2100
(630) 990-6600
www.acehardware.com

Gardener's Supply Company
128 Intervale Road
Burlington, VT 05401
(888) 833-1412
www.gardeners.com

Home Depot
2455 Pace Ferry Rd.
Atlanta, GA 30339
(800) 430-3376
www.homedepot.com

IKEA
www.ikea.com

Lowe's Home Improvement
Warehouse
P.O. Box 1111
North Wilkesboro, NC 28656
(800) 44-LOWES
www.lowes.com

Plow & Hearth
(800) 494-7544
www.plowhearth.com

Restoration Hardware
15 Koch Road, Suite J
Corte Madera, CA 94925-1240
(800) 816-0969
www.restorationhardware.com

Seeds of Change
(888) 762-7333
www.seedsofchange.com

Smith & Hawken
(800) 940-1170
www.smithandhawken.com

Target
(888) 304-4000
www.target.com

True Value Hardware
8600 W. Bryn Mawr Avenue
Chicago, IL 60631-3505
(773) 695-5000
www.truevalue.com

# Recommended Reading

*Classic Roses*
Peter Beales
Harvill Press, 1997
ISBN 1-86046-302-9

*The Complete Guide to Pruning
and Training Plants*
David Joyce and Christopher
Brickell
Simon & Schuster, 1992
ISBN 0-67173-842-9

*Creating Garden Ponds and Water
Features*
Debbie Roberts and Ian
Smith
Laurel Glen, 2001
ISBN 1-57145-492-6

*Creative Vegetable Gardening*
Joy Larkcom
Mitchell Beazley, 2000
ISBN 1-84000-292-1

*Fragrant Gardening*
Steven and Val Bradley
Laurel Glen, 2003
ISBN 1-57145-928-6

*Garden Boundaries*
Toby Buckland
Laurel Glen, 2003
ISBN 1-57145-823-9

*Garden Lighting*
John Raine
Laurel Glen, 2001
ISBN 1-57145-692-9

*Hamlyn Care Manual: Roses*
Amanda Beales
Hamlyn, 2001
ISBN 0-60060-433-0

*Kitchen Harvest*
Susan Berry
Laurel Glen, 2002
ISBN 1-57145-760-7

*The Royal Horticultural Society
Encyclopedia of Gardening*
Christopher Brickell (ed.)
Dorling Kindersley, 1993
ISBN 0-86318-979-2

*The Royal Horticultural Society:
Growing Fruit*
Harry Baker
Mitchell Beazley, 1999
ISBN 1-84000-153-4

*The Royal Horticultural Society:
Pests & Diseases*
Pippa Greenwood and
Andrew Halstead
Dorling Kindersley, 1997
ISBN 0-75130-366-6

## PICTURE CREDITS

**Clive Nichols:** pages 2 (Dinmor Manor, Worcs.), 8/9 (Rupert Golby), 23 (right) (Dinmor Manor, Worcs.), 24/25, 26, 28, 29 (Elisabeth Woodhouse), 36/37 (Eastleach House, Glos.), 38 (Vale End, Surrey), 45 (Rosendal, Sweden), 46/47 (also on back of jacket) (Eastleach House, Glos.), 50, 54 (Wollerton Old Hall, Shrops.), 55 (detail) (Eastleach House, Glos.), 56, 57 (Meadow Plants, Berks.), 60/61, 67 (bottom) (Eastleach House, Glos.), 73 (The Abbey House), 74, front of jacket (Leightholme Dale Lodge, Yorks.).

**Garden Matters:** pages 6 (left), 6 (right), 7 (left), 7 (middle), 7 (right), 15, 19, 20, 23 (left), 30, 31, 32, 34, 40, 44, 49, 51, 52, 63, 65, 67 (top) (detail also on jacket spine), 70, 77 (top), 79, 80/81, 83 (left), 84.

**Derek St. Romaine Photography:** pages 58, 62, 68/69, 77 (bottom), 82, 83 (right).

# Index

Page numbers in *italics* refer to captions